Anderson Boanafina

Course self-evaluation

AF667282

Anderson Boanafina

Course self-evaluation

A methodological proposal for vocational education

ScienciaScripts

Imprint

Cover image: www.ingimage.com

This book is a translation from the original published under ISBN 978-3-330-76082-0.

Publisher:
Sciencia Scripts
is a trademark of
Dodo Books Indian Ocean Ltd. and OmniScriptum S.R.L publishing group

120 High Road, East Finchley, London, N2 9ED, United Kingdom
Str. Armeneasca 28/1, office 1, Chisinau MD-2012, Republic of Moldova, Europe
Printed at: see last page
ISBN: 978-620-8-34292-0

I dedicate this work to God, for the gift of life; to my teachers, for awakening my knowledge and to my family, for their love and support on my journey.

ACKNOWLEDGEMENTS

I thank God and the Enlightened Ones who, by guiding me on the journey of life and in the field of education, have brought me this far. I also thank my eternal and beloved supervisor, Dr Thereza Penna Firme; my parents Nelson and Irene; my siblings; my beloved daughters Mônica and Ana Beatriz; and my beloved wife Lilian, my North, source of inspiration and affection!

SUMMARY

The trend in vocational education today is towards integrating the preparation of citizens for the production process and for life in society, requiring schools to provide teaching based on a solid foundation of scientific knowledge combined with general and cultural training. This reality, which permeates vocational education institutions, strengthens the possibilities of building a new way of responding to social demands for employment and income generation, combating social exclusion and simultaneously promoting the development of science and new technologies. A dilemma then arises in the life of the manager of a public vocational education institution: How can you be sure that your courses are meeting society's demands? One way of answering this question is by subjecting your courses to continuous evaluation processes or, as it will be conceived in this paper, self-evaluation. Thus, from the planning of a new course to its restructuring, managers will have a map of the level of fulfilment of the expectations of their internal consumers (students, staff and those responsible) and external consumers (representatives of the productive world and society in general). The methodological proposal presented here is structured into four evaluation phases and uses Scriven's Consumer-Centred Approach as its theoretical framework. This approach, combined with indicators used by educational sectors, aims to fulfil the essential function of evaluation, i.e. to provide information that helps in decision-making and, more specifically, to produce improvements in the courses evaluated.

Keywords: Self-evaluation. Professional education. Methodology.

SUMMARY

CHAPTER 1

INTRODUCTION

An evaluation process is indispensable to guide any institution seeking to improve its processes, services and/or products. It can even be said that evaluation is an essential support tool for the management of these institutions, both for their development and for achieving high quality standards in their results.

In the public sphere, evaluation plays an important role by contributing to the process of transparency and the implementation of actions that will later have their results reflected in Brazilian society. It is through evaluation that citizens can see how taxes are being converted into benefits.

In recent decades, the consolidation of democracy has helped to increase society's participation in state interventions, whether by demanding austerity from the powers that be in their supervisory role, or by opting for a public university that stands out in external evaluations of its courses, for example. In any case, an accurate and ethical evaluation process is a management tool that helps to combat the waste of resources and, consequently, to meet the demands of society, which finances and consumes public services.

Considering that the consumer of public services is the same as the consumer of private institutions' products and services, according to the principle of equality, these services must maintain a good level of customer service.

It should be emphasised that, even if they do not generate financial profit, the activities carried out in the provision of public services must not consistently frustrate society's expectations and demands to see a return on the taxes paid which, in the dimension of vocational education, can be understood as being the preparation of the individual for employment and/or income generation.

In the case of education, according to Article 205 of the Federal Constitution of 1988 (BRASIL, 1988) and Article 2 of Law No. 9.394 (BRASIL, 1996, Art. 206, Item VII), the Guidelines and Bases Law, the state assumes, together with the family, the duty to educate citizens for life in society based on the principle, among others, of "guaranteeing a standard of quality" in the education provided. With this, the state is obliged to offer public schools in a position to meet society's demands for an education that develops in its citizens the skills needed to exercise citizenship and to work. Therefore, it would not be wrong to say that a public educational institution that does not comply with these principles is neglecting what is recommended by the Federal Constitution and, consequently, the Law of Guidelines and Bases and other legislation that regulates the activities of public bodies.

In this case, a dilemma arises in the life of the manager of a public vocational education institution: How can you be sure that your courses are meeting the demands and expectations of society, as well as the legislation and public policies in force?

One way of answering this question is to subject your courses to continuous evaluation processes, such as the self-assessment conceived in this paper[1] . Thus, from the planning of a new course to its restructuring, the manager will have a mapping of the level of fulfilment of the expectations of its internal consumers (students, staff and those responsible) and external consumers (representatives of the productive world and society in general).

The adoption of an evaluation process helps educational institution managers to understand the behaviour of their courses in the social context, guiding their actions in planning and proposing new actions aimed at training professionals.

An evaluation process (in this case, self-evaluation) also represents a form of accountability to society. Considering that in the majority of government programmes, certain activities that are visible to the population, although efficient in terms of the use of resources, are no longer effective in achieving their objectives.

Self-evaluation should not be instituted as a form of "self-punishment" or "identification of culprits". Self-evaluation should be part of the institutional culture that guides its trajectory and, as a management norm, complete the already universally recognised triad of planning, execution and evaluation.

Understanding the reality before, during and after the implementation of a course will help diagnose the need for essential actions, not as a bureaucratic and incessant activity, but with the aim of being carried out in a timely manner, capable of adapting the public institution to the greater demands of society and its excellence. The challenge lies in creating an evaluation methodology and appropriate indicators that take into account the specificities of vocational education, expressing its responsibility in the formation of human beings, including their values.

The evaluation study presented here, based on the guidelines of current legislation, aimed to develop a methodological proposal based fundamentally on adapting the Criteria of Scriven's evaluation approach (apud WORTHEN; SANDERS; FITZPATRICK, 2004), i.e. "Consumer-Centred Evaluation", to meet the specific needs of the education modality in question, answering the following evaluation questions:

a) Is the proposed course in line with the demands of regional socio-economic development, meeting the demands of citizens, society and the world of work?

b) Is the course in line with the demands identified, the vocation of the educational institution and its real conditions of viability?

c) Does the course respect the identification of professional profiles according to the

[1] The adoption of a self-evaluation is justified because it is an (internal) evaluation process structured and conducted by the very members who participate in and/or are directly affected by the course.

demands identified and in line with policies to promote the sustainable development of the country (region)?

d) Does the course have a curricular and functional organisation in line with the related professional area and the socio-occupational and technological structure?

In this evaluation study, the choice to use a consumer-centred approach is based on the need to obtain data and information from the consumers of a vocational education institution's courses to validate its existence and its relevance to the region in which it operates.

Scriven's approach (apud WORTHEN; SANDERS; FITZPATRICK, 2004) was chosen as the reference for building an approach aimed at vocational education courses because it doesn't provide definitive answers, but rather identifies weaknesses and strengths, looking to the expectations of the different stakeholders to find the way to achieve excellence in vocational training. As a result, all consumers of the course are "heard" and also take on the role of evaluators.

The use of specific indicators for vocational education, associated with the criteria listed by Scriven, aims to identify the degree of fulfilment of the institution's social function, as well as the possible challenges and opportunities for the courses offered.

The aim of this study is to develop an evaluation methodology with specific indicators for the self-evaluation of courses at a public vocational education institution, taking into account the recommendations of CNE/CEB Opinion No. 39 (CONSELHO NACIONAL DE EDUCAÇÃO, 2004). It also discusses the concepts of merit and relevance in the context of course evaluation.

In order to validate the methodological proposal, a self-evaluation process was implemented for a Professional Education Course in the area of Restoration, developed as a pilot project in 2007 at a Public Institution in the State of Rio de Janeiro[2] , which offers professional education in other areas.

The choice of the course in question, among other factors, was due to the need for data and information on how to meet the regional demand for restoration professionals and, consequently, to make a decision on the future of this course, i.e. on whether it should be reorganised, replicated or discontinued.

The relevance of the evaluation study carried out here, through the construction of an evaluation methodology, lies in making the proposal of new courses in public vocational schools more efficient and effective, with the aim of optimising the use of resources and meeting social demands for employment and income.

[2]The identification of the institution has been preserved so that the data and information can be widely used in this study.

CHAPTER 2

PROFESSIONAL EDUCATION: CURRENT CONTEXT

During the 20th century there were nine reforms in secondary education, because as Kuenzer (2000, p. 9-10) points out, it is "the most difficult level to tackle, in terms of its design, structure and organisation". 9-10), it is "the most difficult level to deal with, in terms of its conception, structure and forms of organisation, due to its very nature as a mediation between basic education and vocational training". In other words, on average, secondary education (and technical education within it) is restructured every 11 years, which shows that it is an extremely unstable system, subject to adventures, This demonstrates that it is an extremely unstable system, subject to adventures, fads and isolated actions, far removed from public policies for the educational sphere, based on strategic planning aimed at the country's future in the medium and long term, following the example of countries, today considered to be first world countries, which in the midst of the Industrial Revolution invested in education with a view to development, considering technical education as an important integrated tool and an integral part of a country's economy.

The first movement in favour of changes in the education system took place during the drafting of the 1988 Federal Constitution (BRASIL, 1988), which included articles on the principles that should govern national education and, consequently, the regulation of the functioning of the education system in Brazil. However, it took eight years (1988-1996) of debate and concessions for the new Guidelines and Bases Law (BRASIL, 1996) to be sanctioned and promulgated.

Among the many changes, the Law of Guidelines and Bases, brought Professional Education as complementary to Basic Education, preserving, however, the option of concomitance (in the same or in different educational institutions) during high school, being regulated by Federal Decree No. 2.208 (BRASIL, 1997) .[3]

Chapter III of the Guidelines and Bases Law (BRASIL, 1996) deals with Professional Education, completely changing all the concepts and structures that existed in Law no. 5.692 (BRASIL, 1971) and CFE Opinion no. 45/72, excluding compulsory professionalisation from the structure of regular secondary education and placing it, in addition to educational institutions, in companies and other places where there is competence for such a mission, constituting a parallel education to that considered formal and regular.

In order to regulate §2 of art. 36 and arts. 39 to 42 of the LDB (BRASIL, 1996), Federal Decree 2.208 (BRASIL, 1997, art. 8) was published, outlining the objectives of professional education, establishing the link between technical and preparatory education, determining the levels

[3] This decree was revoked by Decree No. 5.154 (2004), which, among other measures, also integrates vocational education with secondary education. However, its regulation is still being debated.

of professional education, professional qualification, and the organisation of curricula in modules. Creating the link between work and education through the articulation of knowledge (doing, being and living together), generating the competences and skills inherent in the performance of a productive activity.

> [...] competent performance has cognitive, psychomotor and socio-affective knowledge added to it. Competence is essentially characterised by the ability to allocate this knowledge, as resources or inputs, through analysis, synthesis, inference, generalisation, analogy, association, transference, in other words, adapted and flexible **mental schemes**, in actions specific to a specific professional context, generating efficient and effective performance [...] (BRASIL, 1997, p. 7, emphasis added).

With the reform, professional education courses will be able to be organised into modules offering professional qualification for those who complete the course, qualification certification for those who complete a stage or module of the qualification and professional specialisation for those who, on completion of the qualification, undertake a complementary course to their training.

> [...] in the event that the curriculum is organised into modules, these may be terminated for the purposes of professional qualification, in which case they will be entitled to a professional qualification certificate [...] Certificates and diplomas, however, must specify occupational titles that can be identified by the labour market, both in terms of professional qualification and specialisation. For example, in the Health Area: Diploma in Nursing Technician, Certificate of Professional Qualification in Nursing Assistant, Certificate of Professional Specialisation in Occupational Nursing (BRASIL, 1997, p. 32).

To guide institutions in the construction of a new professional education, the National Referentials for Professional Education at Technical Level were presented, embodied in CNE/CEB Opinion No. 16 (BRASIL, 1999a) and CNE/CEB Resolution No. 4 (CONSELHO NACIONAL DE EDUCAÇÃO, 1999b), with its Annex, from the Basic Education Chamber (CEB) and the National Education Council (CNE).

CNE/CEB Resolution No. 4 (CONSELHO NACIONAL DE EDUCAÇÃO, 1999b), which establishes the National Curriculum Guidelines for Technical Professional Education, in its Article 1, sole paragraph, states:

> Professional education, articulated with the different forms of education, labour, science and technology, aims to guarantee citizens the right to the permanent development of skills for social and productive life.

The new legislation therefore becomes flexible and transfers this flexibility to the educational institution, which assumes academic and administrative autonomy and starts to organise its technical courses according to its political and pedagogical project. This was an important break with the old paradigms of Law no. 5.692 (BRASIL, 1971).

In essence, we can see a step forward that makes it possible to build an identity, either through the professional profile or the commitment to the demands of the region that the institution can assume.

Since the LDB (BRASIL, 1996), technical vocational education and secondary education have been guided by two complementary axes: the training of professionals with employability potential and regular preparatory training. The aim of these two axes was to train workers who would be able to build their professional itinerary according to their life project, based on versatility[4] and the enrichment of labour tasks and a more dignified quality of life.

Authors such as Kuenzer (2000) and Ramos (2001) highlight the major contradictions in the LDB which, in its text, by conceiving a character of "flexibility" in professional education, would be maintaining and strengthening social differences, since professional qualification, the minimum necessary to insert a person into the productive world, would reduce public spending in the face of a lack of flexibility,

> [...] quality scientific-technological and socio-historical education for all, a necessary condition for the exercise of citizenship that includes the universal right to participate in the production of material, cultural and political goods [...] (KUENZER, 2000, p. 94).

According to Manfredi (2002, p. 135), the disarticulation of secondary education from vocational training, through Decree No. 2.208 (BRASIL, 1997), would result in the fragmentation of worker training, creating a split in the education system with "[...] the coexistence of separate education networks", one based on propaedeutic logic and the other on market logic.

In fact, social transformations, especially in the 20th century, were associated with a change in the concept of work and the concept of training, influencing the laws that would govern vocational education.

In a brief retrospective, we find that workers at the beginning of the 20th century exercised their profession with only a basic qualification, generally transmitted through experience acquired on

[4] According to Depresbiteris (1999, p. 43-44): polyvalence can be understood: a) in the educational dimension, where the educational system seeks to develop capacity and competences related to problem-solving, autonomy, initiative, creativity, knowledge construction, among others; b) in the productive dimension it can be elementary, aiming at the restricted development of "know-how", by the expansion of tasks, aiming to prepare the worker to develop "activities other than the profession", and by the enrichment of tasks, it is the most complex as it calls for collective participation in production in addition to "changes in knowledge, know-how, know-how and know-how.

an individual basis without any major cognitive complexities, as we saw in the previous chapter. Over the years, production and service techniques have demanded a higher level of qualification, combining learning, aptitude and acquired experience.

As a result, at the end of the 20th century, the dynamics of the productive world demanded that workers be educated instead of simply qualified. In other words, know-how was no longer enough and a body of knowledge was needed, involving not only the learning of techniques, but also the development of interpersonal and intrapersonal behaviour. According to Deluiz (1996, p. 18),

> Work can no longer be thought of from the perspective of a particular job, but of families of occupations that demand similar skills from workers.
> It is therefore no longer a question of a formal qualification/prescribed qualification/qualification of the worker to carry out tasks related to a job, defined by the company to establish salary scales, or by training systems for certification or graduation, where the tasks were described, codified and could be visualised, but of the worker's real qualification, understood as a set of competences and skills, knowledge and know-how, which come from various sources, such as general training (scientific knowledge), professional training (technical knowledge) and work and social experience (tacit qualifications).

This new concept of education marked the end of the 20th century and the beginning of the 21st.

XXI, stirring up debate and criticism from the most diverse currents of thought about the changes they would be imposing on the educational system, especially the professional system.

Critics of the new educational model pointed to the excessive fragmentation of teaching, which consequently caused alienation of the student and subsequently affected their status as workers. A view portrayed by Ney (apud FRIGOTTO; CIAVATTA, 2006, p. 270) when he expressed his opinion on the development of competences in schools.

> The idea here is that each worker, depending on their willpower, merit and ability, will develop professionally, regardless of their professional category. It is interesting to note that in this ideological thinking there is a principle aimed at blaming the worker for his unemployment, which he shares by assuming that he has not prepared himself adequately, that he is less intelligent than someone who is employed, since all the opportunities to succeed in this journey have been made available.

This policy of fragmenting vocational education, as Frigotto, Ciavatta and Ramos (2005) point out, was due to the abdication of an educational policy that favoured integrated training in favour of one that accommodated the needs of the market.

Upon detecting society's demand for a reorganisation of the way vocational education is offered, the Executive repealed Decree no.

2.208 (BRASIL, 1997) and promulgates Decree No. 5.154 (BRASIL, 2004), a Decree that, according to Frigotto, Ciavatta and Ramos (2005), can be considered "hybrid", as it is the result of the clash between conservative forces, which defend the interests of the market, and progressive forces, committed to socio-educational policies that favour the integral formation of the human being. Still according to Frigotto, Ciavatta and Ramos (2005, p. 3), "either we interpret the Decree as a political gain and also as signalling changes [...] or it will be appropriated by conservatism, by the interests defined by the market".

In Cordão's (2005) view, the return of secondary technical vocational education to being articulated and integrated with secondary education does not mean a return to the revoked Law no. 5.692 (BRASIL, 1971), but rather a new concept of education that expands the supply of this type of education to cater for the training of more professionals.

> In relation to the integrated form, [...] it cannot and should not be understood as a course that represents the sum of two distinct, albeit complementary, courses that can be developed in a bipolar way, with one part of general education and another of professional education. This was the logic of the revoked Law 5.692/71. This is not the logic of the current LDB, Law 9.394/96, nor of Decree 5.154/2004, which rejects this dichotomy between theory and practice, between knowledge and its applications. The high school technical vocational education course that is integrated with high school must be considered as a single course from its conception, fully integrated and developed as such from the first day of class to the last. All its curricular components must receive integrated treatment, under the terms of the educational institution's pedagogical project (CORDÃO, 2005, p. 2-3).

CNE/CEB Opinion No. 39 (CONSELHO NACIONAL DE EDUCAÇÃO, 2004), in clarifying the application of Decree No. 5.154 (BRASIL, 2004), identifies criteria that should guide the creation of courses and the establishment of new professional education institutions. This, in a nutshell, is the position of Reporting Councillor Francisco Aparecido Cordão:

> Institutions wishing to start new concurrent courses through an inter-complementary agreement, with unified pedagogical projects and, above all, those adopting the integrated form, will need to have new course plans approved by the respective education systems, as these are new courses, in compliance with Decree 5.154/2004. The criteria for offering technical vocational education courses at secondary level are as follows:
>
> - meeting the demands of citizens, society and the world of work, in line with the requirements of local, regional and national socio-economic development;
> - reconciling the demands identified with the vocation of the educational institution and its real conditions for making the proposals viable;
> - the identification of specific professional profiles for each course, based on the demands identified and in line with policies to promote the country's sustainable development;
> - the curricular organisation of high school technical courses, by professional area, according to the socio-occupational and technological structure (BRASIL, 2004, p.13).

These criteria served to guide the construction of the Indicators, with their respective standards, on which this work is based.

CHAPTER 3

ASSUMPTIONS ABOUT EVALUATION

An unsystematic or informal evaluation occurs instinctively, according to Belloni (2000, p.14), forming part of our daily lives as an "[...] instrument of survival for any individual or group". However, an action that seeks to understand facts, explain phenomena, propose improvements, quantify data or qualify them begins to follow rules, pre-established conditions that will guide its trajectory towards the proposed objective, becoming considered a systematic or formal evaluation, as Belloni, Magalhães and Sousa (2000, p. 186) argue,

> [...] it is possible to develop an evaluation system aimed at improving the quality of education - that is, teaching, learning, research and institutional management - with the aim of transforming today's school into an institution geared towards and committed to the democracy of knowledge and education, as well as the transformation of society.

A reflection on the development of the conceptual field of evaluation cannot fail to consider the evolution and dynamics of social life, considering that, as a social practice, evaluation has permeated the historical construction of humanity since its inception. Those who assess have a relationship of power with those being assessed. According to Dias Sobrinho (2002, p. 17), "the conceptual field is permeated by power, it is a bundle of contradictions of conceptions, values and interests and of struggles by groups to secure places and positions".

The evaluation process involves technical and methodological aspects, but has ethical, political and cultural concepts at its core, as it is centred on the participation of people. As such, its results reflect the social environment in which it is carried out, loaded with its own values, in other words, it is not neutral.

The evaluation activity could be described as a constant competition between the legitimacy of data collection and the representativeness of its results. The strategies and resources used by evaluators in this dispute form different visions of the most valued and recognised evaluation practices.

Scriven (1991, p. 3) defends the importance of evaluation when he describes it as,

> [...] a science insofar as it involves the production of knowledge rather than art, jokes, or plays. [...] Science itself is only distinguishable from pseudoscience by evaluating the quality of the evidence, research models, instruments, interpretations.

A brief analysis of the historical trajectory of evaluation practice shows an evolution from measuring, measuring, observing and describing reality to critical analysis with an ethical-political value judgement agreed between those involved. As a result, the results of the evaluation became of interest not only to the evaluators, but also to those involved in the evaluation processes (the stakeholders). According to Dias Sobrinho (2002, p. 21),

> [...] evaluation at this time continues to be markedly technical, but is no longer simply identified with measurement. More than that, assessment is referred to as a process of continuous improvement of a programme and is turned towards the reformulation of curricula, the establishment of educational objectives to be met, individual differences and the constitution of regional or national standards.

This complexity, which constitutes the act of evaluation, leads the evaluator to immerse himself in the process in order to understand the multiple internal and external interferences that affect the result. According to Grinspun (2001, p. 228), any evaluation of learning, public policies or programmes "seeks to engage in a productive dialogue between theory and practice, between policy and action, between subjectivity and objectivity", which affect human beings and/or institutions.

For Guba and Lincoln (1989 apud PENNA FIRME et al., 2009) it was only a few decades ago that scholars really began to discuss evaluation in a more conceptual way, its instruments, means, interpretations, applicability and results, both inside and outside the educational system.

Penna Firme and others (2009, p. 172) argue that it is necessary to differentiate between the concepts of evaluation policy and evaluation culture, because while the former "is perceived as a set of guidelines that establishes rules and procedures [...], evaluation culture is part of the set of [...] beliefs, values, styles and behaviours [...]" of organisations. In the author's opinion,

> Evaluation is usually a challenge for both the evaluator and the evaluated. [...] the presence of an evaluation culture makes it easier to face this challenge, its absence often generates fear of evaluation. [...] Carrying out an evaluation in an area with no evaluation policy and no evaluation culture is chaotic [...] (PENNA FIRME et al., 2009, p.173-174).

The evaluation culture in Brazil is generally built after the implementation of evaluation processes based on the experiences of other institutions. However, once it has been appropriated by those involved, the evaluation process makes it possible to guide decisions in a rational way and, from an understanding of its essence, to build relationships between the institutional mission with its actions and these with its products and/or services offered to society.

In universities, the culture of evaluation tends to contribute to improving the quality of their courses and generally gives rise to integrative actions, as defined by Lopes and Silva (1998, p. 52),

> In the view of the academic community, it has stood out not only for the direct results produced in terms of analyses and reflections on teaching, research, extension and management, but also for the learning generated about the meaning of the institution

> and the establishment of an identity that is transformed to meet social changes in the regional community and beyond.

In a country full of contradictions and marked, on the one hand, by the cartorial life typical of the 19th century citizen and, on the other, by the knowledge society typical of the 21st century, the culture of evaluation is becoming an important tool for educational institutions, helping to reveal and improve educational actions, including courses, which can include the socially excluded.

By permeating these two parallel universes that coexist in our society, education brings together members who, paradoxically, are alienated from the productive context by the same elements that weave the speed of regional economic development. In this context, evaluation appears in educational practice as an element that promotes institutional knowledge.

Institutional evaluation, when it focuses on its courses, emerges as a management tool that enables decision-making and the development of strategies that, in addition to contributing to the process of differentiating the services offered, lead to the perpetuation of the institution. These are challenges that are closely related to the institution's operational and political issues, but which need to be overcome if professional education is to create a flexible behaviour and a competitive stance in the regional and national context, aiming for quality in the courses offered.

The proposal to evaluate courses in the context of education is recent, but it is already being used by higher education managers both to guide the expansion of their courses and in the academic and administrative reform of the institutions themselves. However, its practice is still not widespread in basic and professional education.

The benchmark for starting an evaluation process in education is the dissemination of its institutional mission. From this point on, all the evaluation phases, from planning to the final report, will in fact be geared towards meeting the objective of knowing or verifying the real situation of the institution. According to Kotler (1998, p. 88) "the mission statement must be a motivating guide for employees and must be strongly linked to the organisation's competences". This means that in order to evaluate a course you need to make sure that everyone involved knows as clearly as possible what the purpose of its existence is and how it relates to the mission of the institution in which it is located.

This clarity will make it possible to create channels of communication and information between the interested parties (stakeholders) who, directly or indirectly, are the ones who will truly be affected by the results of the actions implemented by the educational institution and, consequently, by the outcome of its evaluation.

Achieving a common vision of the institutional reality on the part of those involved is an indispensable aspect for the planning and success of their courses. For Penna Firme (2004, p. 4-5), in his article The Advances of Evaluation in the 21st Century,

> [...] the evaluation process will have to penetrate the merit of its object as an internal value, implicit and independent of any applications; and more broadly discover its relevance, as it is useful in its results, repercussions and impacts. Evaluation in its broadest sense is therefore a challenge and, in order to achieve it, creativity and sensitivity, objectivity and subjectivity are present and active, whenever necessary, in order to respond appropriately to enquiries and facilitate improvement action.

The ongoing evaluation process allows for discussion about the direction of the institution and, consequently, reflection on the options that lead to the improvement of the services provided, identifying the specific challenges for the advancement of each of the Courses and, consequently, the changes that may be necessary. As Penna Firme (2004, p. 18) defines in his article: "[...] the excellence of the evaluation process lies in being useful in the information it offers, feasible in the realisation of its trajectory, ethical in its purposes and consequences and precise in the elaboration of its instruments and treatment of its data".

In general, it should be checked whether the evaluation process is useful to the institution, generating reliable and fruitful results; viable in its implementation, as a feasible process and by the adherence of those involved; accurate in the construction of representative indicators; and ethical in the transparency of the process, valuing the participants as active but also passive subjects of the act of evaluation.

Evaluation in education should not be confused with a form of standardisation of courses or state control, but rather a search for quality in the provision of services. A moment to identify the path of merit and social relevance.

On the same principle as higher education, the evaluation of vocational education courses will promote a new collective awareness among public managers and society of the need for constant improvement in the search for merit and relevance to society.

The merit of the public institution concerns the efficiency, efficacy and effectiveness of the structure available to its courses, so that they have a positive impact on their target audience. Relevance consists precisely of the importance that the results produced by the educational institution have in improving the social context, either by building and disseminating scientific knowledge and technological development or by increasing the population's employability and income generation potential.

A course evaluation, based on the set of indicators, is a "gauge" of performance in relation to its objectives. These indicators are defined as "a comparable set of information that allows the diagnosis of the situation under study, whether global or partial" (BRASIL, 1994, p.15).

With a mission to be born and live within the social context of its region, vocational education is an integrating part of the multiple aspects of society, whether in the political, cultural, legal, organisational, socio-economic and/or support for regional sustainability, through local opportunities.

One of the most common mistakes made by managers is trying to replicate vocational education courses as a model in different social contexts without first analysing the region. Only by getting to know the social reality is it possible to address it more proactively and thus design a course that meets its demands.

The evaluation process, in the context of professional education, goes beyond the internal institutional dimension because it subsidises decisions that will affect society. It (the evaluation process) is not "self-limiting and self-sufficient", to quote Dias Sobrinho and Balzan (2000, p. 95), but leads to reflection on the relevance of the courses and even the very existence of the institution.

Understanding and accepting their limitations and challenges, which are just as important as the solutions themselves, must take into account that an excessively short-sighted and endogenous view of superiority causes a loss of sensitivity to social change.

Even though there is no single model for course evaluation, especially self-assessment, it needs to be systemic, considering that all agents, internal or external, can influence the performance of courses and the institution itself. Thus, having indicators about the region where the programme is located and its situation in relation to similar programmes contributes to operational balance and strategic expansion.

Course evaluation helps the institution to generate and manage information and data that characterises it as it is. In this way, the impacts of possible changes, be they institutional policies or (infra)structure, will be softened and managed more easily.

Similarly, an internal evaluation process, conducted by the institution's own evaluator(s), will be able to identify the challenges more clearly. According to Penna Firme, Tijiboy and Stone (2001), the immersion[5] of the evaluator in the evaluation context is beneficial, as they interact with the environment in such a way that they become invisible and can observe without any "masks" interfering with their evaluation. In the same vein, listening to students, managers, the internal community and productive circles (the real evaluators) will help improve the courses offered and to be offered.

The perception of quality, based on the results of the internal evaluation, will be geared towards the concept of integrating people with the processes and systems that run through the institution, in other words, by internalising concepts that reflect the image of an institutional identity that works in a synchronous and planned way, through actions that make it possible for its Courses to be inserted sustainably into the social space destined for institutions recognised for their educational excellence.

In this process of building excellence, "merit in the intrinsic qualities of the programme; and relevance, in its results, its impact, its influence, in what was worthwhile" (PENNA FIRME, 1994,

---

[5] Lectures given at the Specialisation Course in Educational Assessment, at UERJ, in November 2001.

p.15), are the main aspects to be assessed.

For Stufflebeam (1993 apud COTO, 2007, p. 46),

> Evaluation is a process of identifying, collecting and presenting useful and descriptive information about the value and merit of the goals, planning, realisation and impact of a given object, in order to guide decision-making, solve accountability problems and promote understanding of the phenomena involved.

3.1 SOME EVALUATION APPROACHES

In the quest to understand phenomena, researchers and scholars from different areas of knowledge use evaluative approaches as mechanisms to identify, collect, understand and measure reliable data pertinent to their field of research, with the aim of producing useful information.

Among the different evaluation approaches, Worthen, Sanders and Fitzpatrick (2004) classify them into six categories:

A) Objective-centred approach - which focuses on specifying goals and objectives and determining the extent to which they have been achieved;

B) Management-centred approach - whose central interest is in identifying and meeting the information needs of managers who make decisions;

C) *Expert-centred approach* - where the approach basically relies on the direct application of professional expertise to judge the quality of whatever activity is being assessed;

D) Opponent-centred *approach* - where the planned opposition, in terms of the different evaluators' points of view, pros and cons are the central focus of the evaluation;

E) *Participant-centred approach* - which calls for the involvement of the participants, who are interested in the object of the evaluation, to determine the values, criteria, need and data of the evaluation

F) *Consumer-centred approach* - this approach considers the well-being of a programme's target audience (consumers) as the main justification for its implementation. This approach seeks to determine the merit and relevance of the programme in relation to the benefits generated for consumers.

Regardless of the approach chosen, the essential function of evaluation is to provide information that will also help managers or other *stakeholders* make the decisions they deem appropriate. This is how Stufflebeam's well-established concept of evaluation as a process that provides useful information for decision-making emerged in 1966.

3.2 INDICATORS IN THE FIELD OF EDUCATION

Indicators are defined as "a comparable set of information that allows the diagnosis of the situation under study, whether global or partial" (BRASIL, 1994, p.15). They are mechanisms that help evaluate and control the results or performance of an action that is to be measured. By collecting data and information, they make it possible, for example, to assess the progress made with the results obtained from the implementation of an institution's quality improvement programmes. They reveal aspects of a given reality through probable variations.

In the context of evaluation, indicators are the basic and essential reference point for guaranteeing a dimension that is both particular and comparable between processes. This property of being articulated transcends the evaluative moment and, when indicators are well constructed, ensures their reliability and reference.

Thus, it will be up to the evaluator or researcher to analyse the indicators and, associated with the set of observations and/or contextual information, assign relevant considerations. Quoting Minayo (2009, p. 84),

> [...] they are quantified or qualitative parameters that serve to detail whether the objectives of a proposal are being carried out well (process evaluation) or have been achieved (results evaluation).

The analyses provided by the indicators can be carried out from various angles, specifically showing the behaviour of a segment and/or the institution as a whole.

The challenge in constructing indicators is to have them portray a given situation in a simple way, despite the uncertainty and complexity that often surround them. To be considered valid, according to Jannuzzi (2002, p. 54), "it is necessary to ensure that there is, in fact, a reciprocal relationship between the indication (concept) and the proposed indicators".

Authors such as Jannuzzi (2002) and Minayo, Assis and Souza (2005, p. 3) attribute to indicators an important relationship between the planning, evaluation and formulation of social policies in the different spheres of government, "their function is only to be a signpost: indicators are instruments, they do not operate on their own, they indicate what they should indicate".

According to Penna Firme, Tijiboy and Stone (2001, f. 11), when indicators are "defined by practice", the evaluator is able to group together common "manifestations" of groups defined as the focus of the evaluation. In a representative way, these indicators can be followed over time in order to understand the results or impacts caused by interventions on the group under study. Thus, through the presence or absence of variations in these indicators, the evaluator will have the opportunity to meet specific expectations.

The indicators constructed from the evaluator's observation are important elements when the object of the evaluation is a social programme. They serve to "measure" the merit and relevance of interventions in certain contexts or social groups for whom the programme is intended.

Penna Firme, Tijiboy and Stone (2001) emphasise that the difference between indicators defined on a theoretical basis and those based on the evaluator's practice lies in the fact that the former is defined in advance and, in the field, directs the collection of the corresponding data. On the other hand, in the second case, the definition of indicators begins with the evaluator's immersion in the evaluation context, identifying what the aforementioned authors define as "clues" and then, in later stages, defining the indicators that are pertinent to the context and objective of the evaluation.

As there are no indisputable indicators, the only way to be representative is to formulate reasonable proposals that can, by consensus among those involved, be accepted as a standard of measurement in specific contexts, with the sole condition that valid indications are derived from their application, in order to evaluate in the right direction, according to the concept taken as a basis.

More broadly, Valarelli (apud MINAYO, 2009, p. 129) refers to theoretical studies on indicators through recommendations such as:

- be built in the context of a negotiation process and based on the vision and conception that the various actors involved have of the central objectives of the evaluation;
- consider the specificities of the context;
- define the effects attributable to the interventions being evaluated;
- be orientated towards learning and understanding processes;
- foresee and specify the means of verification;
- be simple and understandable for everyone, not just specialists;
- be viable from an operational and financial point of view;
- to provide relevant information for decision-making;
- take advantage of information from reliable sources, saving the group resources, time and energy.

The authors cited so far agree on the need to build simple evaluation processes, based on objective indicators and

representative. In this sense, its clear understanding by those involved will help structure an evaluation process whose results will be accepted as the first step in proposing improvement and development actions. According to Penna Firme, Tijiboy and Stone (2001), the important thing is that the indicator is capable of capturing changes when they exist.

Therefore, when defining indicators for evaluating courses, identifying consumers' perceptions, expectations and criticisms is fundamental to realising the social function of public professional education. In this way, the definition of indicators arises both from theoretical references, validated by previous experiences, and from the evaluator's experience in the context of professional education.

For the educational evaluator, the choice and use of indicators, more broadly, will correspond to the degree of proximity between the concept of the indicator and the measure, i.e. its ability to actually reflect the abstract concept it sets out to identify, such as efficiency, efficacy, effectiveness, sustainability, merit, relevance, the impact of the Course on the social context in which the institution is inserted or the rates of graduates employed in reputable companies in the market.

The most convenient and representative arrangement of quantitative and qualitative indicators in a self-evaluation process will depend on the aspects you want to analyse. Varelli (apud MINAYO, 2009) recommends that, in the case of educational evaluation, it is necessary to consider, among other factors:

- conceptions, interests and approaches of the organisations and actors involved - good indicators emerge from those involved
- context in which the indicators must be specified, representing the evaluative reality
- management mode as:

> [...] The way an evaluation proposal is organised must include a clear project, with objectives and goals, basic concepts, a connection between the different researchers and other actors, and methodological designs in their broadest sense (often requiring quantitative and qualitative approaches) (VARELLI apud MINAYO, 2009, p. 85).

- resources using indicators that can be applied over time and are available.

The definition of useful and precise indicators, with the aim of analysing processes and producing improvements, represents a strategic advance in the consolidation of an evaluation culture within educational institutions. These are the first steps towards educational quality which, from an institutional point of view, is based on building and adding value to the services they (institutions) provide. And for this to be fully successful, the political skill of the manager is fundamental when designing and implementing the evaluation process, which will consequently organise the purposes and procedures for building constant improvements in their institution.

Society's tendency is to focus on the material, tangible and quantifiable results of educational institutions. If the manager of a vocational education institution limits himself solely to these indices and ignores the opinion of the community, he will lose the systemic vision of the context in which his institution is inserted and who its Courses serve.

CHAPTER 4

COURSE SELF-EVALUATION: A METHODOLOGICAL PROPOSAL

The evaluation methodology presented here was structured on the basis of Scriven's Consumer-Centred Evaluation Criteria (apud WORTHEN: SADERS; FITZPATRICK, 2004). An approach that considers the user of products or services to be the main reference point for assessing the quality and relevance of what is being offered.

To make it easier to visualise the methodology developed, a summary table has been drawn up (from section 4.4.1 onwards) in which the Scriven criteria are associated with factors and indicators specific to the assessment of vocational education courses by stage.

4.1 A BRIEF OVERVIEW OF CONSUMER-CENTRED EVALUATION

According to Scriven (1991), evaluation should provide sufficient information to support judgements about the merit and value of the components of a programme and of activities carried out and to be carried out, with the aim of producing results. As well as defending the value judgement as an important part of the act of evaluation, Scriven states that it is not enough to report on the success of a programme, for example. According to the author, the evaluator needs to be concerned about its effects, as these could raise important questions for the target audience (consumer).

Scriven (1991) defined evaluation as judging the value or merit of something. This value judgement can be made either from comparison standards, which can be the result of applying criteria and norms, or from scientific procedures. However, the result will always depend on the choice of instruments and, above all, the most appropriate indicators for the evaluation process.

In Scriven's definition of evaluation (apud WORTHEN: SADERS; FITZPATRICK, 2004), merit refers to the intrinsic value of the evaluation, as opposed to extrinsic or system related value. He combated the idea of simply using evaluation as an instrument to monitor whether or not objectives were met and proposed the Goal Free Evaluation Model which, according to the author, helps:

> 1. To avoid the risk of focusing only on the stated objective of the programme and thus ignoring important unexpected results;
> 2. To remove the negative connotations associated with the appearance of unexpected, collateral or secondary results. As well as unforeseen effects or even a tendency to put on the back burner what should be considered crucial, especially in terms of new priorities;
> 3. To eliminate prejudices and introduce concepts whose goal is already known;
> 4. To maintain the objectivity and independence of the evaluator (SCRIVEN apud WORTHEN; SANDERS; FITZPATRICK, 2004, p. 274-275).

For Scriven (1991), evaluation has the function of verifying what has been achieved in terms of benefits for the programme's target audience (consumer), determining its (the programme's) merit and establishing a relationship between its effects and the needs of the target audience (consumer), guiding actions to achieve success. According to Scriven (1991, p. 23), the evaluation process should include "[...] formative evaluation, which is carried out throughout the process with the introduction of changes, and summative evaluation, carried out after the end of a process to verify the results".

The author also stresses the need for the objective of the programme itself to be the object of evaluation, and defends the argument that the evaluator should obtain, through a variety of instruments, as much information as possible about the object involved in the evaluation process so that, based on standards of comparison, they can structure a value judgement. It can be considered that the most proficient evaluator of a product or service is the consumer themselves.

In Cronbach's (1963) view, evaluating the internal structure of a programme is more important than making a comparison with other programmes (DIAS SOBRINHO, 2003). The contributions of Cronbach, Scriven and Stufflebeam (apud WORTHEN; SANDERS; FITZPATRICK, 2004, p. 166), among other theorists, brought a new vision to the consumer-centred evaluation approach:

> The summative role of assessment, he said, [enables] administrators to conclude whether or not the entire ready-made curriculum, refined by the use of the assessment process in its [...] formative role, represents a significant enough advance over the existing alternatives to justify the expense of its adoption by a school system.

In the evaluation process of a programme, summative evaluation is generally one-off and takes place at the end of a period in order to determine whether or not the previously established objectives have been met, generating information so that decisions can be made on whether to continue, improve or end the programme. Formative evaluation, on the other hand, is designed to provide information on development, with the aim of adjusting the process to the objectives (WORTHEN; SANDERS; FITZPATRICK, 2004).

Consumer-centred evaluation considers the well-being of its target audience and, regardless of the programme, seeks to determine its merit and relevance in relation to the benefits generated. The origin of this approach lies in the need to generate information about "educational and other social welfare services" (WORTHEN; SANDERS; FITZPATRICK, 2004, p.165). Thus, evaluation has a dual purpose: to obtain information during the action in order to monitor it (formative evaluation) and to make decisions about the process and results achieved by this evaluation (summative evaluation).

In the consumer-centred approach, stakeholders in the programme interact by taking on the role of the subject of their own evaluation. As a result, they gain a greater understanding of the programme, make better decisions and increase the quality of their products.

4.2 THE STRUCTURE OF THE METHODOLOGICAL PROPOSAL

The construction of the indicators, and of the evaluation methodology itself, calls for a review of approaches characteristic of relevant bibliographical and documentary studies.

The main indicators used by educational sectors that already have course evaluations were analysed, using those from the Curriculum Guidelines for Vocational Education and information sources such as: from the Anísio Teixeira National Institute of Pedagogical Studies (INEP); from the Brazilian Institute of Geography and Statistics (IBGE); from the Rio de Janeiro Information and Data Centre Foundation (CIDE Foundation); from the Rio de Janeiro State Education Council; from the Rio de Janeiro Secretariats of Education and Science and Technology and from sector reports (such as specialised publications containing data and information from official sources).

This evaluation was structured taking into account

A) CNE/CEB Opinion No. 39 (CONSELHO NACIONAL DE EDUCAÇÃO, 2004) - Application of Decree No. 5.154 (BRASIL, 2004) in Technical Professional Education at secondary level and in Secondary Education, in the identification of criteria and in the construction of indicators for professional education;

B) CNE/CEB Resolution No. 04 (CONSELHO NACIONAL DE EDUCAÇÃO, 1999), which establishes the National Curriculum Guidelines for Professional Education at Technical Level

C) Scriven's "Consumer-Centred Evaluation Approach" (apud WORTHEN; SANDERS; FITZPATRICK, 2004) - for determining the factors and their indicators used in the approach to self-evaluation, incorporating them into the methodology in the evaluation phases:

- Diagnostic phase - with the aim of obtaining initial information (inputs) to identify the region's natural and productive vocations, social demands, profile and the need or otherwise for the course in the region. Its product will be the information and data base for implementing the courses.

At this first stage, the evaluator must ascertain the real situation, the challenges and opportunities, and draw up an action strategy. This phase focuses on potential consumers. It is carried out through market observations and consultations with "input indicators", which are useful for sizing up the necessary resources.

- Formative phase - with the aim of providing periodic information (process) on the execution of the Course, avoiding accumulations of problems and losses in the focus of work, these are carried out through observations, tests, conversations and consultations using "process indicators" to quantify the performance of activities related to the way goods and services are produced.

- Summative phase/1 (product) - with the aim of comparing the planned Course and its performance in execution. in human resources and/or infrastructure.

- Summative phase/2 (results) - at the end, evaluating the results can, where necessary, lead to improvements in the method, content and profile,

The use of "output indicators" shows the results produced by the course, while "outcome indicators" point to the consequences of implementing the course.

In the summative phase, the indicators were developed to identify the challenges of the previous phases and contribute to solving a particular problem or meeting a demand from society.

In each of these phases, the manager can make decisions[6] to correct distortions, if any, or programme complementary actions that will contribute to the success of the course.

As the development of the evaluation depends on the participation of consumers of the school's product (the Course), for the purposes of understanding this work we used the definition of consumer in the Consumer Defence Law, Law No. 8.078 (BRASIL, 1990, Art. 2), as being "any natural or legal person who acquires or uses a product or service as the final recipient", as well as empirically creating four categories of local consumers of vocational education institutions:

1) The productive world - represented by companies (public and/or private) and income-generating opportunities which, as consumers, use the knowledge developed and the professionals trained in vocational education courses;

2) The students - consumers of the services provided by the educational institution, i.e. the course taught and the educational projects carried out;

3) Society - the consumer of the products and services developed by the professionals (graduates of the courses) working in public or private companies, who are consequently players in the regional development process;

4) Education professionals - consumers of the job opportunities generated by the vocational education institution itself, for managers, teachers, technical-pedagogical staff and support staff.

4.3 COURSE SELF-EVALUATION

In accordance with CNE/CEB Opinion No. 39 (CONSELHO NACIONAL DE EDUCAÇÃO, 2004), the proposed indicators are related to the criteria, with their respective factors, from Scriven's list (apud WORTHEN; SANDERS; FITZPATRICK, 2004, p.167), representing the process of: setting up the course, assessing its viability; putting the course into practice, assessing its real usefulness in meeting demands; and the results, assessing the accuracy of the content and resources applied in the course.

The methodological design proposed by the author adapted the list of Criteria developed by Scriven (apud WORTHEN; SANDERS; FITZPATRICK, 2004), objectives, objects, indicators,

[6] Planning (mapping), deployment (structuring), implementation (execution) and revision (correction).

sources, expected results and specific target audience/consumers to meet the needs of vocational education courses. These Criteria are also grouped into four phases - Diagnostic, Formative, Summative/1 and Summative/2, as shown below:

4.3.1 First Phase of Self-Assessment - Diagnostic Phase

In the first phase of self-evaluation, the evaluative function should express a diagnosis of the inputs needed to implement and develop the course, i.e. the regional profile, social demands and the feasibility of investments.

The set of indicators should provide the manager with information and data to respond to the criterion, established in CNE/CEB Opinion no. 39 (CONSELHO NACIONAL DE EDUCAÇÃO, 2004, p. 10) for professional education, of "meeting the demands of citizens, society and the world of work, in line with the requirements of local, regional and national socio-economic development".

These indicators should provide the manager with information and data to answer the following Evaluation Question in the Diagnostic Phase:

- Is the proposed course in line with the demands of regional socio-economic development, meeting the demands of citizens, society and the world of work?

Table 1 below presents a Matrix linking the Scriven Criteria and Factors to the Indicators, Data Collection Sources, Expected Results and Target Audience/Consumer proposed in this evaluation for the Diagnostic Phase.

Criteria	Factors	Indicator	Sources	Expected results	Target Audience/Consumers
	Evidence of need	Number of vacancies in the productive sectors	IBGE, DIEESE, FIRJAN, trade unions and local market research	Local production profile	Public and private companies in the region and opportunities to generate income
	Relevance Social	Quantitative target audience, resident in the region, in the age group and/or schooling and/or social condition necessary to attend the Course	PNAD School Census (MEC/INEP) IBGE (CENSUS/PNAD)	Mapping the regional target audience	Audience defined by profile
Need	Number affected	Number of people enrolled in schools, number of people registered in social projects and/or employment reference centres in the region)	School Census (MEC/INEP); Ministry of Labour records; Assistance segment registers.	Mapping by segments of the region	Potential candidates for the course

	Lack of a replacement	Number of institutions and enrolments in similar vocational courses	School Census (MEC/INEP)	Mapping of institutions and enrolment in vocational courses similar to the one proposed	Public and private vocational education institutions in and around the region
Market	Size and importance of potential markets	Number of places on offer	IBGE, DIEESE, FIRJAN, trade unions and local market research	Identification of job vacancies and income-generating opportunities	Public and private companies in the region and opportunities to generate income
Cost benefit	Cost benefit	Cost of a similar course	Course Project/ Suppliers	Lower cost associated with better performance per course	Students

Table 1. Diagnostic Assessment: Inputs. Source: The author (2009).

4.3.2Second Phase of Self-Assessment - Formative Phase

In the second phase of self-evaluation, the formative function of the evaluation should express the process of implementing and developing the course, i.e. consumer feedback on the course in progress. This phase should be repeated annually with a view to improving the course.

The set of indicators should provide the manager with information and data to respond to the professional education criterion of "identifying specific professional profiles for each course, based on the demands identified and in line with policies to promote the country's sustainable development".

In order to obtain data, questionnaires were developed for students, graduates, teachers, managers and representatives of the productive sectors (ANNEXES A, B, C and D).

This phase refers to the evaluation of the process which, consequently, in the context of an educational institution is directed at its Courses, as it aims to identify assertiveness and possible inaccuracies that can be corrected, preferably while the Course is still running.

The set of indicators should provide the manager with information and data to answer the following Evaluation Question in the Formative Phase:

- Is the course in line with the demands identified, the vocation of the educational institution and its real conditions of viability?

Table 2 below presents a Matrix linking the Scriven Criteria and Factors to the Indicators, Data Collection Sources, Expected Results and Target Audience/Consumer proposed in this evaluation for the Formative Phase.

Criteria	Factors	Indicator	Sources	Expected results	Target Audience/Consumers
Performance - authentic consumer	Consumer satisfaction	Level of consumer satisfaction	Self-evaluation questionnaires Interviews Suggestions/complaints Market research	High level of satisfaction with the course in progress	Students/ Teachers/ Professionals from the Institution Representatives of the productive segments
Performance - authentic consumer	Suitability	Number of trainees hired per year	School secretariat Partner companies	100% success rate for trainees	Trainee students
Performance critical comparisons	Level of competitiveness	Enrolment rate Number of classes from competing institutions	School Office School Census (MEC/INEP)	Outperforming competitors	Competing institutions
Performance - side effects	Results	Unemployment Indices: Structural, Conjunctural and Frictional	IBGE, DIEESE, FIRJAN, Ministry of Labour and local market study	Low unemployment rates related to Courses	Productive world
Performance - real field experiments	Meeting demands	Level of effectiveness of the curriculum and infrastructure Degree and experience of the course's teaching staff Relationship between degree and experience	Curriculum matrix, contents, teaching qualifications and existing infrastructure	High performance in meeting social demands	Society
Cost benefit	Investment efficiency	Cost Index Student	Institution management	Lower cost associated with better performance per course	Student
Performance - process	Course Acceptance	Enrolment rates Offer of internship/job vacancies Comparative employability index of the institution's graduates	School Office Internship Centre	Increase in enrolment and internship/job vacancies	Society Representatives of the productive segments

Table 2. Formative Assessment - Process. Source: The author (2009).

4.3.3 Third Self-Assessment Phase - Summative Phase/1

In the third phase of self-evaluation, the summative function of the evaluation should represent the opinion of consumers on the efficacy and effectiveness (impact) of the products of vocational education institutions.

This phase, like the previous one, should be repeated every year with a view to improving the course and the set of indicators should provide the manager with information and data to respond to the professional education criterion of "curricular organisation of high school technical courses, by professional areas, according to the socio-occupational and technological structure".

For this phase, questionnaires were developed to evaluate the institutional structure and the opinion of graduates.

This phase refers to the evaluation of the product which, after the end of the course, contributes to analysing its development and the level of satisfaction and criticism of the graduates towards the institution and the course.

In this phase, the same questionnaires were used as in the previous phases, due to the special situation in which the entire evaluation process took place when the course had already been completed.

The set of indicators should provide the manager with information and data to answer the following Evaluative Question in the Summative Phase/1:

- Does the course respect the identification of professional profiles according to the demands identified and in line with policies to promote the sustainable development of the country (region)?

Table 3 below shows a matrix linking the Scriven Criteria and Factors to the Indicators, Data Collection Sources, Expected Results and Target Audience/Consumer proposed in this evaluation for the Summative Phase/1.

Criteria	Factors	Indicator	Sources	Expected results	Target Audience/Consumers
Performance - statistical relevance	Effectiveness	Enrolment, pass, retention, dropout and school flow rates	School Office	Low retention and drop-out rates. High enrolment, pass and school flow rates	Students
	Effectiveness (social impact)	employability rate of its graduates index of Comparative employability of the institution's graduates	School Office Employers Trade Unions	100% integration of graduates into the productive world	Graduates
Performance - causal model	Effectiveness	Level of institutional competence	Questionnaire applied to graduates	High level of professional fulfilment	Graduates
	Recognition	Course Utilisation	School Office	100% success	Graduates

	Social	Index Comparative employability index of the institution's graduates	School Census (MEC/INEP)	rate at school High employability rate	
Performance - educational relevance		Number of: Patents; Publications and Service contracts	Institution Management/ CNPq/ Funding Bodies/ INPI	Growth in the institution's scientific, technological, academic and professional output	Teachers, Students and Professionals of the Institution

Table 3. Summative Assessment - Product.

Source: The author (2009).

4.3.4 Fourth Self-Assessment Phase - Summative Phase/2

In the fourth phase of self-evaluation, the summative function of the evaluation should represent the results needed to analyse the previous phases, checking for possible critical points.

This phase should be implemented with a view to improving the institution as a whole.

The set of indicators should provide the manager with information and data to respond to the professional education criterion of "reconciling the demands identified with the vocation of the educational institution and its real conditions for making the proposals viable"

For this phase, questionnaires were developed to evaluate the institutional structure and the opinion of graduates.

This phase refers to the evaluation of the results, and is carried out after the end of the Course and the analyses of the previous stages of the self-evaluation, with the aim of improving the structure of the Course before the start of the next one.

In this phase, the same questionnaires were used as in the previous phases, due to the special situation in which the whole evaluation process took place when the course had already been completed.

The set of indicators should provide the manager with information and data to answer the following Evaluative Question in the Summative Phase/2:

- Does the course have a curricular and functional organisation in line with the related professional area and the socio-occupational and technological structure?

Table 4 below shows a matrix linking the Scriven Criteria and Factors to the Indicators, Data Collection Sources, Expected Results and Target Audience/Consumer proposed in this evaluation for the Summative Phase/2.

Criteria	Factor	Indicator	Sources	Expected results	Target Audience/Cons

					umers
Broadening the support base	Institutional development	student to teacher ratio	School Office	Get closer to a ratio of between 15 and 17 students per teacher	Student Lecturer
	Institutional quality	Course Teaching Staff Qualification Index	Supporting documents	Increase in the qualifications and experience of the course's teaching staff	Lecturer
	Proficiency	Proposals resulting from diagnosis, process and product phases	Results of the diagnosis, process and product phases	High institutional performance	The Professional Education Institution

Table 4. Summative Assessment - Results. Source: The author (2009).

4.4 FORMULAE USED IN THE PROPOSED INDICATORS

The proposed indicators were constructed on the basis of the author's observations, secondary data collection, consultations with official sources and documentary information and references. However, some of the data, which originates from the educational institution itself, needs to be organised for the purposes of analysis and comparison. Based on this realisation, the author of this paper prepared (and adapted) a set of formulas with the aim of obtaining seven indices that would help in the self-evaluation of the course.

When calculating the indices, it should be noted that the "students" or "graduates" of a course come from the sum of all the classes (of the same course) that started and finished simultaneously. So, for example, if a school started three nursing courses in 2007, the graduates would be the graduates of those three courses, including students from internal or external transfers.

a) Employability index of the institution's graduates - (IE) and (lEc)

a.1) Simple (IE)

Objective: To quantify the rate of graduates in employment in relation to the total number of students graduating in the same year.

Definition: The number of graduates corresponds to the total number of students who have completed their courses and internships (if required), and are able to enter the labour market and find employment. Graduates are all students who are completing the course and graduates.

Calculation method:

$$I.E = \frac{\text{Graduates employed (year x)}}{\text{Graduating students (year X)}}$$

Scale: 0 to 1 = 0 being the lowest level and 1 the highest level of institutional performance (insertion) in relation to the demands of the productive world.

Reference indicator: Employment Rates and Sectoral Studies.

a.2) Compared - (IEc)

Objective: To quantify the rate of employed graduates in relation to the total number of employed workers, with the same level and course of training, in the region.

Definition: The number of graduates employed corresponds to the total number of graduates, in the same year per course, who were employed in companies in the region. Employed workers correspond to the total number of workers, with the same level and course of study as the "employed graduates", who entered the labour market in the region in the same year.

Calculation method:

$$I.Ec = \frac{\text{Graduates employed (year x)}}{\text{Workers employed (year X)}}$$

Scale: 0 to 1 = 0 being the lowest level and 1 the highest level of institutional performance (insertion) in relation to the demands of the productive world.

Reference indicator: Employment Rates and Sectoral Studies.

b) Retention Index - (IRFE)[7]

Objective: To quantify the retention rate in relation to the total number of students.

Definition: The number of students in each year corresponds to the total enrolment in the same year per course. Dropouts are those students who, during the course of their studies, left the course (transfer and abandonment);

Calculation method:

$$IRFE\ (\text{year X}) = \frac{\text{Total Number of Students (Retained + Withdrawn + Dropped Out) (year x)}}{\text{Total Students Enrolled (year x)}} \times 100$$

Scale: 0 to 100% = 0% being the lowest level and 100% being the highest level of retention. Retention is understood to be a weakness that the institution needs to correct.

Reference indicator: 0% retention rate.

c) Course Faculty Titration Index (ITC)

Objective: To quantify the Degree Index of the Teaching Staff - Permanent and Substitute - who teach theoretical and practical classes on the course.

Definition: The qualifications of the teaching staff are divided into 5 sub-groups: Technicians (T), Graduates (G), Specialists (E), Masters (M) and Doctors (D).

Calculation method:

$$ITC = \frac{T*1+G*2+E*3+M*4+D*5}{T+G+E+M+D}$$

[7] Adaptation of the document: Calculation Methods for the Management Indicators of the Federal Network of Professional and Technological Education (EPT) determined in Ruling 2.267/2005-TCU - same observation for items: c and d.

Scale: corresponds to an index for monitoring teaching qualifications, i.e. an increase in the variant is associated with an increase in teaching qualifications

Reference indicator: largest ITC

Note: The ITC could become an indicator for external evaluation, as an element in the qualification of the institution's teaching, pedagogical and administrative staff.

d) Student Cost Index (ICA)

Objective: To quantify the institution's cost/student ratio per course, making it possible to identify investment in student training.

Definition: All expenditure was taken into account, except for investment, capital, precatory payments, inactive and pensioners. The number of students in each year corresponds to the total enrolment in the same year per course.

Calculation method:

$$ICA = \frac{\text{Total Investment per Course}}{\text{Total Enrolment by Course}}$$

Scale: corresponds to an index for monitoring the cost of the course, i.e. an increase in the variant is associated with an increase in the cost of student training per course. The student cost used as a reference for this study is R$3,203.00[8] (INEP, 2005, p. 81), which basically includes the same items mentioned in the "Investment Efficiency" Factor table in the course's formative assessment phase.

e) Course Utilisation Index - (IAC)

Objective: To quantify the course completion rate in relation to the number of initial enrolments.

Definition: The number of students entering each year (or term), per course, corresponds to the total enrolment. The number of Course completers corresponds to the total number of students who, after the regular time of the Course, have managed to complete all the subjects and internship practice (if any).

Calculation method:

$$IAC = \frac{\text{Total Course Graduates} \times 100}{\text{Total Initial Course Enrolment}}$$

Scale: 0 to 100% = 0% being the lowest level and 100% being the highest level of achievement. 100 per cent of the course is understood to be the institution's objective.

Benchmark: 100 per cent pass rate for the course.

[8] According to data from the Survey of the cost per pupil per year in basic education schools that offer quality education: 2ª stage (INEP, 2005).

f) Student to teacher ratio - (IAD)

Objective: To quantify the number of students per course in relation to the number of teachers per course.

Definition: The number of students per course corresponds to the total enrolment. The number of lecturers on the course corresponds to the total number of lecturers who teach theoretical and practical classes on the course.

Calculation method:

$$IAD = \frac{\text{Total Initial Course Enrolment}}{\text{Course Teachers (Theory + Practice)}}$$

Scale: corresponds to the direct relationship between enrolment and number of teachers per course

Reference indicator: Between 15 and 17 students per teacher in vocational education courses. Reference School Census 2007 and Social Indicators (UNDP).

CHAPTER 5

APPLYING THE SELF-ASSESSMENT MODEL

This chapter presents the self-evaluation of the Professional Education Course in the area of Catering, as mentioned above, applying the methodology developed by this author.

Qualifying professionals is one of the biggest challenges in recovering memory, mainly due to the lack of educational institutions and professionals to train new professionals.

Among the international agreements, the document entitled "Convention Concerning the Protection of the World Cultural and Natural Heritage" (UNESCO, 1972, p. 1), organised during the seventeenth session of the General Conference of the United Nations Educational, Scientific and Cultural Organisation, held in Paris in 1972, warns nations about the risks of erasing our past, according to the document:

> [...] cultural heritage and natural heritage are increasingly threatened with destruction not only due to natural causes of degradation, but also to social and economic development aggravated by even more worrying phenomena of alteration or destruction.

In its Article 5 (UNESCO, p. 3-4), the Convention states that:

> In order to ensure effective protection and conservation and to actively valorise the cultural and natural heritage located in its territory and under conditions appropriate to the countries, each State Party to this Convention shall endeavour to:
> a) adopt a general policy aimed at giving cultural and natural heritage a role in collective life and integrating its protection into planning programmes;
> [...]
> c) developing studies, scientific and technical research and perfecting methods of intervention that enable the state to deal with dangers to cultural or natural heritage;
> [...]
> d) encourage the creation or development of national or regional training centres for the protection, conservation or enhancement of cultural and natural heritage and stimulate scientific research in this field.

In Brazil, the Ministry of Culture, through the National Institute of Historical and Artistic Heritage (IPHAN)[9] and together with state and municipal heritage protection and preservation institutions, has been developing actions to promote research and the development of specialised

---

[9] IPHAN, the federal body that served as the basis for the establishment of state and municipal bodies for the protection of cultural heritage, was created by Decree No. 25 of 30 November 1937, drawn up by Mário de Andrade at the request of Gustavo Capanema, minister of then president Getúlio Vargas, and is still in existence today. Together, the properties listed by these three bodies - federal, state and municipal - preserve a sample of significant Brazilian cultural production, from its origins to the present (BRASIL, 2008).

professionals. And, through the Monumenta programme, it promotes and finances the restoration and recovery of listed properties and the training of specialised restoration workers.

The pilot project for the course in question was made possible using public funding, with the aim of training professionals in restoration, primarily for 48 young people aged between 16 and 22 who live in the area surrounding the educational institution.

The self-evaluation process was carried out in an environment that historically associates the demands of society with technological development and this with education, resulting in teaching that is recognised as being of excellence. In this way, the evaluation process will enable not only a systemic view of the course offered, but also the implementation of an evaluation culture that analyses the context in which it was generated and implemented and, if necessary, adjustments to the course with a view to its continuity and replication in other spaces.

5.1 COURSE SELF-EVALUATION

Course evaluation is important because it enables the internal community and society to understand the dimensions that permeate professional training, be it the objectives, mission or identity of the institution in focus, strengthening vocational education in Brazil, its historicity and legislative frameworks.

The construction and improvement of evaluation instruments that include benchmarks makes it possible to systematise and incorporate an evaluation culture that guides the institution's actions. In order to fulfil this evaluation practice, two groups of instruments were developed:

a) an instrument with closed questions, used to verify the physical, pedagogical, human resources and results structure of the institution (ANNEX A).

b) three instruments, with open questions, used to obtain data and information with the aim of building indicators to help plan, implement and evaluate the Course (ANNEXES B, C and D).

To obtain the necessary information, they were identified and selected as participants in the evaluation:

- 01 technical course coordinator;
- 03 course teachers;
- 32 students graduated from the course;
- 03 representatives from the productive world.

5.1.1 Profile of Self-Assessment Consumers

Defining the profile of the consumers of an organisation's services or products is the first and most important step towards excellence. Four categories of local consumers were used in this evaluation:

A) The productive world - understood to be the consumer of the knowledge developed at the school and in its laboratories, either through its graduates, who join public or private companies to produce, or through the products and services generated directly by the institutions. Thus, in this evaluation, it is represented by companies in the restoration sector.

B) students / graduates - are understood to be the consumers of the services provided by the educational institution, i.e. the classes taught and the educational projects carried out. Thus, in this evaluation, they are the 48 young people aged between 16 and 22 who live in the low-income communities surrounding the institution.

C) society - understood to be the direct consumers of the products and services developed by the professionals (graduates) who work in public or private companies, and the indirect consumers who benefit from the taxes generated by regional development. Thus, in this evaluation, they are the 144,000 residents of the communities surrounding the institution, according to data from the 2000 Census (IBGE, 2003).

D) professionals from the institution - these are understood to be consumers of the job opportunities generated by the vocational education institution itself, from managers, teachers, technical-pedagogical staff and support staff. Thus, in this evaluation, it is the institution's professionals who work on the course.

In the present self-assessment, which was carried out after the end of the Course, the questionnaires were applied simultaneously to the Consumers identified above, as follows:

A) For the graduates, the questionnaires were sent by e-mail to the 37 graduates of the class of 2007, who were considered approved, but only 4 replied by e-mail. After three attempts to contact them by e-mail, 15 graduates answered the questionnaires by telephone, totalling 19 responses out of the 37 initially planned;

B) For the teachers, the questionnaires were applied directly to 2 teachers and sent to 1 by e-mail, who did not reply;

C) For the representatives of the production world, 3 companies specialising in the construction and/or restoration sector were selected, only one of which replied to the questionnaire sent by email.

D) The questionnaire was administered directly to the course coordinator.

Even with the limitations in the return of the questionnaires sent out, the responses, combined with the observations of the context in which the course is inserted, were considered satisfactory and representative, contributing to the construction of the scenario necessary for the proposed evaluation.

5.1.2 General Course Information

Course: Basic Professional Qualification in Conservation and Restoration of Immovable Cultural Property - Stucco and Mural Painting.

Start and end of course activity: 2007

Mode: Face-to-face

Level of Professional Education: Initial and Continuing Training for Workers

Course Workload: 540h

Of which: 270 hours of lectures and 270 hours of supervised practice in projects

In numbers: 16 teachers; 48 students enrolled; 02 classes; shifts (M and T)

At the end of the course:

Successful students: 37 (77%)

Retained students: 07 (14.5%)

Dropouts: 04 (8.5%)

5.1.3 Questionnaire applied

The questionnaires were designed to help the members of the internal evaluation committee map out general but relevant information that could influence the development of the course.

One caveat. Considering that the evaluation took place two years after the end of the course, the questionnaires were adapted to this reality, without prejudice to capturing the information necessary for the proposed self-evaluation model. (Models of the questionnaires applied are in the ANNEXES).

5.2 SELF-EVALUATION RESULTS

The results presented here are organised to answer each of the four questions guiding the evaluation, corresponding to each of the Evaluation Phases - Diagnostic, Formative, Summative/1 and Summative/2.

5.2.1 First Phase - Diagnostic

This phase corresponds to the diagnosis of the necessary inputs for the implementation of the course, with the aim of providing support for the decision on its realisation.

The set of indicators should provide the manager with information and data to understand whether the course being evaluated is in line with the demands of regional socio-economic development, meeting the demands of citizens, society and the world of work.

The diagnosis of the region's productive, demographic and educational profiles was used as a source for this phase, in accordance with Table 1, presented above, structured on the basis of the Criteria and Factors from Scriven's list (apud WORTHEN; SANDERS; FITZPATRICK, 2004, p.167).

I) Criterion: "Need"

A) Factor: "Number affected/preferred audience"

A total of 4,966 young people between the ages of 16 and 22 enrolled in secondary education at public schools in the region were identified

B) Factor: "Social relevance / target audience"

A total of 7,194 young people were identified, living in the region, aged between 16 and 22, in or with secondary education.

C) Factor: "Lack of replacement"

No similar courses were identified in or around the region.

D) Factor: "Evidence of need"

Evidence of the need for the course in the region was seen on the IPHAN website (BRASIL, 2008). It is important to emphasise that in the state of Rio de Janeiro there are countless historic monuments in need of conservation and restoration, with two works in progress and fourteen proposals under analysis in 2009.

II) Criterion: "Market"

A) Factor: "Size and importance of potential markets"

Identifying job vacancies and income-generating opportunities is extremely difficult, especially as it is a demand that generally depends on:

- approval, from the project to its execution, by various official bodies;
- investments, usually high, of public or private resources that don't always converge in financial gains or political interest;
- specific professional qualification
- technological development
- high cost of raw materials

III) Criterion: "Cost-effectiveness"

A) Factor: "Comparative cost-benefit"

No cost of the same or similar institutions or courses in or around the region was identified for comparison.

The actual initial investment for the course in question was R$550,331.15 (2007). This amount refers to: the project; the building; permanent and consumable material; outsourced services and scholarships.

Considerations in the diagnostic phase:

It was not possible to establish a comparative relationship between the cost of implementation, due to the lack of similar ones in the region, nor was direct evidence found between the proposed course and the requirements of regional socio-economic development, i.e. the set of indicators used to assess the inputs did not identify possibilities for employment or immediate income generation for the residents of the region analysed.

5.2.2 Second Phase - Formative

This phase corresponds to the evaluation of the process which, in the context of the course being evaluated, aims to identify assertiveness and possible flaws that can be corrected, preferably while the course is still running.

The set of indicators should provide the manager with information and data to understand whether the course being evaluated is in line with the demands identified, with the vocation of the educational institution and with its real conditions of viability.

The answers to the questionnaires were used to fulfil the following criteria, in accordance with Table 2, presented above, structured on the basis of the Criteria and Factors from Scriven's list (apud WORTHEN; SANDERS; FITZPATRICK, 2004, p.167).

IV) Criterion: "Performance - authentic consumer"

A) Factor: "Consumer satisfaction"

A.1) Consumer: Graduates (19)

- What challenges and opportunities did you face after taking the course?

Challenges: Access to internships or jobs in the field for 100 per cent (19)

Opportunities: Having had experience with restoration projects for 78.9% (15)

Keeping up to date for 15.7% (3)

Not for 5.4% (1)

- In your opinion, do the subjects and contents of the course make it possible to train professionals to meet the needs of the market? If not, what do you think would be necessary?

Yes to 100% (19)

- In your opinion, has the infrastructure offered by the institution made it possible for your training to meet the needs of the market? If not, what would need to be changed/invested in so that it does?

Yes to 100% (19)

It is worth highlighting the respondents' reservations:

"infrastructure is still a target for improvement" for 5.4% (1)

"even though it's in a really small place" for 5.4% (1)

a.2) Consumer: Teachers (2)

• In your opinion, graduates will have employment or income-generating opportunities?Please justify your answer.

Yes to 100% (2)

Justifications: "The course aims to train a professional who is increasingly scarce in the labour market" for 50% (1)

"The course offered good training" for 50 per cent (1)

• In your opinion, do the Curricular Matrix and Programme Contents of the Course enable the training of professionals to meet the demands of social agents (private and public companies, NGOs, etc.)? If not, what would need to be changed in order to meet them?

Yes to100% (2)

It is worth highlighting the respondents' reservations:

"With specific regard to the ornamental stucco technique, the course offers theoretical and practical content that enables the training of a professional who meets the demands of the labour market. [...] The course and its curriculum were designed to meet the demands [...]" for 50% (1)

• In your opinion, does the infrastructure offered by the institution make it possible to train professionals to meet the demands of social agents? If it doesn't, what would need to be changed/invested in so that it does?

Partially to 100% (2)

Suggestions: a drawing room; space for mural painting classes; teachers' room; computer room; specialised library; acquisition of furniture; suitable equipment; expansion of the creative space.

• How do you rate it?

• the course curriculum (justify):

Adequate to the profile of the course offered for 100% (2)

• the professionals (teachers, technical-pedagogical team, management, coordination) who work on the course (justify):

Very good for 50% (1)

Good for 50% (1)

• Did you participate in the conception and/or implementation of the course? How?

Yes 100% (2) - content, content suggestions, handouts

• Suggestions/Criticisms/Comments:

Referring students for internships

Increased course hours

Inclusion of Portuguese language

Environmental subject

a.3) Consumer: Productive World (1)

- Are you satisfied with the professionals working in your company today?

Yes to100% (1)

<u>It is worth highlighting the respondents' reservations:</u>

"although they need training, or rather specialisation/updating"

- In your opinion, what would need to be added to professional training in order to meet the demands of the service?

Technical and theoretical training courses in the area of listed heritage

B) Factor: "Suitability"

Since 2007, 5 (10%) trainees have entered the market

V) Criterion: "Performance - critical comparisons"

A) Factor: "Level of competitiveness"

There is no competitor in the region, and the enrolment rate and number of classes are zero

VI) Criterion: "Performance - side effects"

A) Factor: "Results"

No sectoral studies were found for this area, so structural, cyclical and frictional unemployment rates cannot be assessed.

VII) Criterion: "Performance - authentic field experiments"

A) Factor: "Meeting demands"

A.1) Consumer: Productive World (1)

- What is the minimum level of education required to fill these vacancies?

"High School"

- Are there any difficulties in filling vacancies (if so, list some reasons)?

"Yes, it's a profile in training - usually a student (higher education), with a committed schedule"

- III) Criterion: "Cost-benefit - a comprehensive analysis of the cost-benefit ratio"

A) Factor: "Investment efficiency"

Note: The items listed below were identified in the sector reports consulted as being generally applicable to budgeting a course. However, in this evaluation, of the twelve items, seven did not have their values identified, as the institution did not have separate data for each course.

	Item	R$
1	Educational material	-
2	Consumables	6.009,00
3	Laboratory equipment	-
4	Human resources	-

5	Scholarships (Student Financial Aid)	74.881,00
6	Maintenance	-
7	Publicity / selection process	-
8	Consultancy/lectures	-
9	Transport/ per diems	-
10	Commercial (Individuals)	1.855,00
11	Services (Legal Entities)	61.401,00
12	Other:	20.278,00
	Total	164.424,00

Table 5. Budget Source: The author (2009).

Note: Cost:

(1) per class: R$ 82,212.00 (2 classes)

(2) per student: R$ 3,425.50 (48 students)

IX) Criterion: "Performance - process - presentation of evidence of product use"

A) Factor: "Course Acceptance"

- Vacancies offered = 48
- Number of applicants for selection = 360 (class year 2007)
- Enrolment rate = 48
- Internship vacancies = 05
- Job offer = 01
- The institution's Employability Index = 0.02

Formative phase considerations:

According to the set of indicators, even if it doesn't meet regional demands and it's not possible to compare it with others, the course is in line with the institution's vocation and its real conditions of viability.

The student cost used as a reference for this study is R$3,203.00 (CORDÃO, 2005, p. 81)[10] , which basically includes the same items mentioned in the "Investment Efficiency" Factor table. However, as not all of the values were identified in the course being evaluated, especially the Human Resources item (salaries and wages), it can be considered that the student cost of R$3,425.50 practised in the course being evaluated is higher.

The reservations, criticisms and suggestions made by consumers should guide the changes aimed at improving them.

5.2.3 Third Phase - Summative/1

This phase corresponds to the evaluation of the product which, after the end of the course, contributes to analysing its development and the level of satisfaction of its graduates. In order to collect information, the same questionnaires were used as in the previous phases, due to the special

[10] According to data from the Survey of the cost per pupil per year in basic education schools that offer quality education: 2ª stage (INEP, 2005).

situation in which the whole evaluation process took place (with the course already finished).

The set of indicators should provide the manager with information and data to check whether the course being assessed respects the identification of professional profiles according to the demands identified and in line with policies to promote sustainable development in the region, in accordance with Table 3, presented above, structured on the basis of the Criteria and Factors from Scriven's list (apud WORTHEN; SANDERS; FITZPATRICK, 2004, p.167).

X) Criterion: "Performance - statistical relevance"

A) Factor: "Institutional effectiveness in combating school dropout and retention"

- Enrolment = 48
- Approval rate = 77.1 %
- Retention rate = 14.5%
- Dropout rate = 8.5%
- Retention rate = 22.9%

B) Factor: "Effectiveness (social impact)"

The employability rate of graduates is 0.02 (01 Hired)

XI) Criterion: "Performance - causal model"

A) Factor: "Effectiveness (level of graduate satisfaction)"

a.1) Consumer: Graduates

- How do you rate it?
- <u>the subjects of the course (justify):</u>

Excellent for 52.6% (10)

Very good for 36.8% (7)

Good for 10.6% (2)

- <u>the professionals (teachers, technical-pedagogical team, management, coordination) who work on the course (justify):</u>

Excellent for 89.4% (17)

Very good for 10.6% (2)

- How would you rate the quality of teaching in the course?

Score Ten for 52.6% (10)

Score Nine for 42.2% (8)

Score Eight for 5.2% (1)

- How would you rate the institution's infrastructure?

Score Ten for 36.8% (7)

Score Nine for 52.6% (10)

Score Eight for 10.6% (2)

• Suggestions/Criticisms/Comments:

Predominance for:

Increase in course hours to 47.3% (9)

Referral of students to internships and/or jobs for 78.9% (15)

Other answers quoted:

Air conditioning

Fan

More space

Laboratories

Computer Room

a.2) Productive world consumer

• In your opinion, does the profile of the professionals in the area who work for your company meet what you want? If not, what do you consider to be the right professional profile for the job?

"No. People with experience"

• What is the desired level of training for professionals working in the area in question?

"All levels. It depends on the work"

XII) Criterion: "Performance - educational relevance"

A) Factor: "Social recognition (social impact)"

It was not possible to calculate the comparative employability rate of the institution's graduates because there is no data on similar courses in the region

B) Factor: "Social recognition (institutional effectiveness)"

It was not possible to map patents; publications and/or service contracts carried out by the institution under evaluation because there is no data on similar courses in the region.

Considerations of the Summative Phase/1:

It was not possible to identify a relationship between the professional profile, in terms of the demands identified, and the policies to promote sustainable development in the region where the course is located.

The course showed an excellent level of acceptability by the graduates, but the level of retention (or failure) was high (22.9%), and a more specific assessment is needed of the causes that produced this rate.

5.2.4 Fourth Phase - Summative/2

This phase corresponds to the evaluation of the results carried out after the end of the course, with the aim of improving the structure of the course before starting a new class.

The same questionnaires were used as in the previous phases, as a result of the special situation in which the whole evaluation process took place (course already completed).

The set of indicators should provide the manager with information and data to analyse whether the course being assessed has a curricular and functional organisation in line with the related professional area and the socio-occupational and technological structure required by the region's productive segments, in accordance with Table 4, presented above, structured on the basis of the Criteria and Factors from Scriven's list (apud WORTHEN; SANDERS; FITZPATRICK, 2004, p.167).

XIII) Criterion: "Broadening the support base - plans made for after data collection and programme improvement"

A) Factor: "Institutional Development"

The student-to-teacher ratio for the course in question is 3:1 (three students for each teacher), with 48 students for 16 teachers.

B) Factor: "Institutional quality"

The degree/training index of the course's teaching staff has a profile of:

- Technical 12.5% (2)

. Graduate 37.5% (6)

- Specialist 6.2% (1)
- Master 43.8% (7)
- Doctor 0% (0)

Course Faculty Index = 2.8

It was not possible to verify the professional teaching experience of the professionals involved in 2007

C) Factor: Institutional proficiency

The main proposals resulting from the evaluation processes of the process and product phases are:

- Increased course hours
- Development of a school-company integration programme to promote the course and make internship and job vacancies possible.

Considerations of the Summative Phase/2:

The course's curricular and functional organisation is in line with the related professional area and the institution's socio-occupational and technological structure. It is necessary to review the distribution between theoretical and practical workloads, as well as its integration with companies operating in the area.

As an action, consideration should be given to the possibility of on-site visits to construction sites, as well as to companies operating in the sector, with the aim of drawing up a matrix of competences and skills needed to train professionals. In this way, there will be harmony between the course proposals and the demands of the productive world.

The main proposals resulting from the evaluation processes of the process and product phases are:

- Increased practical course hours
- Development of a school-company integration programme to promote the course and make internship and job vacancies possible.

CHAPTER 6

FINAL CONSIDERATIONS

Brazil has a population growth rate of 1.3% per year, representing the prospect of a country with a young population. However, the high illiteracy rate, which according to IBGE data (2008) is between 10% and 12%, represents a significant indicator of the exclusion of sections of the population from access to and permanence in the school system. This illiteracy rate, for example, is a far cry from countries classified as developed, such as Sweden and the USA, with rates of less than 1.0%.

When comparing the rate of secondary school enrolment, Brazil (65.4%)[11] is close to Mexico (66.1%), much higher than Nigeria (29.5%), but much lower than the USA (96.3%) and Sweden with universal secondary education. These factors consequently influence the number of professionals dedicated to research and technological development[12] - two fundamental elements for a country's economic and social growth, both in terms of adding value to products and services and the population's quality of life.

Vocational education gives millions of young people access to a solid general education combined with technology and culture. That's why this type of education needs, more than preparatory education, special investments targeted by demand, guiding its expansion to places where there are few or no opportunities for employment and income generation, contributing to the creation and expansion of productive sectors.

However, vocational education isn't just that, it's more than teaching how to produce, it's an education where there is technological development, science and the production of knowledge, so it's also aimed at those who have had access to the best schools, at the right time in their lives and who bring, as a vocation, the desire to build, to save lives, to transform realities and to discover the future.

REFERENCES

BELLONI, I. The social function of institutional evaluation. In: SOUSA, E.C. B. M. (Org). Institutional evaluation. 2. ed. Brasília, DF: Ed. UnB, 2000.

BELLONI, I.; MAGALHÃES, H.; SOUSA, L. C. Metodologia de avaliação em políticas públicas: uma experiência em educação profissional. São Paulo: Cortez, 2000.

BRAZIL. Constitution (1988). Constitution of the Federative Republic of Brazil. Brasília, DF: Federal Senate, 1988.

. Decree No. 2.208, of 17 April 1997. Regulates § 2 of art. 36 and arts. 39 to 42 of Federal Law no. 9.394/96, which establishes the Guidelines and Bases of National Education. Legislation, Brasília, DF, 17 April 1997. Available at: <http://www.crprj.org.br/legislacao/documentos/ decreto1997-

11 Yearbook and Database of the UNDP, WHO, UNESCO, ILO, UNICEF, UNIFPA and the World Bank (JANNUZZI, 2002).

12 The ratio of professionals dedicated to science and technology in Brazil is 0.3 people per thousand inhabitants, while in Sweden the ratio is 6.8.

2208.pdf>. Accessed on: 5 May 2009.

. Decree no. 5.154, of 23 July 2004. Regulates § 2 of art. 36 and arts. 39 to 41 of Law no. 9.394, of 20 December 1996, which establishes the guidelines and bases of national education, and makes other provisions. Federal Official Gazette, Brasília, DF, 26 July 2004.

______. Law no. 5.692, of 11 August 1971. Establishes Guidelines and Bases for 1st and 2nd grade education, and makes other provisions. Official Gazette of the Federative Republic of Brazil, Brasília, DF, 12 August 1971.

______. Law no. 9.394, of 20 December 1996. Establishes the guidelines and bases of national education. Official Gazette of the Federative Republic of Brazil, Brasília, DF, 23 December 1996.

______. Ministry of Culture. IPHAN. Brasília, DF, 2008. Available at: <http://portal.iphan.gov.br/portal>. Accessed on: 3 Feb. 2008.

______. Ministry of Education. Secretariat for Higher Education. Programme for the Institutional Assessment of Brazilian Universities. Brasília, DF, 1994.

CASTRO, M. H. G. Education for the 21st century: the challenge of quality and equity. Brasília, DF: INEP, 1999.

NATIONAL EDUCATION COUNCIL. Chamber of Basic Education. CNE/CEB Opinion No. 16, of 5 October 1999. National Curriculum Guidelines for Technical Professional Education. Official Gazette of the Federative Republic of Brazil, Brasília, DF, 26 November 1999a.

NATIONAL EDUCATION COUNCIL. Chamber of Basic Education. CNE/CEB Opinion No. 39, of 8 December 2004. Application of Decree No. 5.154/2004 in Technical Professional Education at secondary level and in Secondary Education. Brasília, DF, 8 December 2004. Available at: <http://www.idep.ac.gov.br/docs/legfed/parecer39_04.pdf>. Accessed on: 20 March 2009.

. CNE/CEB Resolution no. 4, of 8 December 1999. Establishes the National Curriculum Guidelines for Technical Professional Education. Official Gazette of the Federative Republic of Brazil, Brasília, 22 December 1999b. Section 1, p. 229.

CORDÃO, F. A. Professional education in Brazil. In: PONTIFÍCIA UNIVERSIDADE CATÓLICA (SP). Postgraduate Studies in Education Programme. Secondary education and technical education in Brazil and Portugal: historical roots and current panorama. Campinas, SP: Autores Associados, 2005.

COTO, M. J. A. Modelos de evaluación. *Revista Universitarà de Sociologie,* n. 2, 2007. Available at: <http://cis01.ucv.ro/revistadesociologie/files/rus-2- 2007.pdf#page=40>. Accessed on: 27 July 2009.

CRONBACH, L. J. Course improvement through evaluation. Teachers College Record, New York, n. 64, p. 672-683, 1963.

DELUIZ, N. Economic globalisation and the challenges for vocational training. Boletim Técnico Senac, Rio de Janeiro, v. 22, n. 2, p. 15-21, May/Aug. 1996.

DEPRESBITERIS, L. Current conceptions of vocational education. Brasília, DF: SENAI/DN, 1997. (SENAI Series. Training for Trainers).

DIAS SOBRINHO, J. Democratic evaluation. Florianópolis: Insular, 2002.

DIAS SOBRINHO, J. (Org.). Evaluation and public commitment. Florianópolis: Insular, 2003.

DIAS SOBRINHO, J.; BALZAN, N. C. (Org.). Avaliação institucional: teorias e experiências. São Paulo: Cortez, 2000.

FRIGOTTO, G.; CIAVATTA, M. (Org.) A formação do cidadão produtivo: a cultura de cercado no ensino médio técnico. Brasília, DF: INEP, 2006.

FRIGOTTO, G.; CIAVATTA, M.; RAMOS, M. A política de educação profissional no governo Lula: um percurso histórico controvertido. Educação e Sociedade, Campinas, SP, v. 26, n. 92, p. 1087-1113, oct. 2005.

GRINSPUN, M. P. S. Z. Institutional evaluation. Ensaio: avaliação e políticas públicas em educação, Rio de Janeiro, v.9, n. 31, apr./jun. 2001. Available at: <http://www.scielo.br/pdf/ea/v4n10/v4n10a05.pdf>. Accessed on: 7 May 2009.

IBGE. Census 2000. Rio de Janeiro, 2003.

IBGE. Synthesis of social indicators: an analysis of the living conditions of the Brazilian population 2008. Rio de Janeiro, 2008 (Estudos e pesquisa. Informação demográfica e socioeconômica, 23).

INEP. Survey of the cost per pupil per year in basic education schools that *offer quality education*: 2ª stage: report

national research. Brasília, DF, 2005. Available at: <http://www.publicacoes.inep.gov.br>. Accessed on: 22 March 2009.

JANNUZZI, P. M. Indicadores sociais na formululação e avaliação de políticas públicas. Revista Brasileira de Administração Pública, Rio de Janeiro, v. 36, n. 1, p. 51-72, jan./feb. 2002.

KOTLER, P. Marketing management: analysis, planning, implementation and control. 5. ed. São Paulo: Atlas, 1998.

KUENZER. Secondary and vocational education: the policies of the neoliberal state. 2. ed. São Paulo: Cortez, 2000.

LOPES, F. D.; SILVA, I. B. UNIJUÍ: uma experiência de avaliação institucional participada. Avaliação: revista da Rede de Avaliação Institucional da Educação Superior, Campinas, SP, v. 3, n. 2, 1998.

MANFREDI, S. M. Professional education in Brazil. São Paulo: Cortez, 2002.

MINAYO, M. C. Construction of qualitative indicators for evaluating change. Revista Brasileira de Educação Médica, Rio de Janeiro, v. 33, n. 1, p. 83-91, 2009. Available at: <http://www.scielo.br/pdf/rbem/v33s1/a09v33s1.pdf>. Accessed on: 7 July 2009.

MINAYO, M. C.; ASSIS, S. G.; SOUZA, E. R. (Org.). Avaliação por triangulação de métodos: abordagem de programas sociais. Rio de Janeiro: Ed. FIOCRUZ, 2005.

PENNA FIRME, T. Evaluation today: perspectives and trends. In: NATIONAL SYMPOSIUM ON EDUCATIONAL EVALUATION: a critical reflection. Proceedings... Rio de Janeiro: Cesgranrio

Foundation, 1994.

______. The advances of evaluation in the 21st century. Rio de Janeiro, 2004. Available at: <www.cenpec.org.br/modules/editor/arquivos/c8a0633f-4d01-eae6.pdf>. Accessed on: 26 June 2008.

PENNA FIRME, T. et al. Evaluation culture and evaluation policy as guides to practice: reflections on the Brazilian experience. Ensaio: avaliação e políticas públicas em educação, Rio de Janeiro, v.17, n. 62, p. 169-180, 2009.

PENNA FIRME, T.; TIJIBOY, J. A.; STONE, V. I. Evaluation of social programmes: how to approach it and how to put it into practice. Rio de Janeiro, 2001. Mimeographed.

RAMOS, M. N. The pedagogy of competences: autonomy or adaptation? São Paulo: Cortez, 2001.

SCRIVEN, M. Evaluation thesaurus. 4th ed. Newbury Park, CA: Sage, 1991.

UNESCO. Convention Concerning the Protection of the World Cultural and Natural Heritage. In: GENERAL CONFERENCE, 17, 1972, Paris. Papers presented... Paris, 1972.

Available at: <http://www.dominiopublico.gov.br /download/text/ue000114.pdf>. Accessed on: 3 Feb. 2008.

WORTHEN, B. R.; SANDERS, J. R.; FITZPATRICK, J. L. Programme evaluation: concepts and practices. Translation by Dinah de Abreu Azevedo. São Paulo: Ed. Gente, 2004.

ANNEXES

ANNEX A - Questionnaire Template for Situational Analysis Fill in one questionnaire per Course

Name of course:

Modality:

Start of course: Completion:

Professional Education Level:

C/h: h (h theory + h supervised practice)

Total: teachers ( ); students ( ); classes (); shifts ( )

Students Passed: Retained: Dropped Out:

Please note: Fill in the questions with multiple answers and quantities where necessary.

Part 1 - Teacher Profile

a) Regarding teaching activity - the number of teachers who:

Item	Quantity
a.1 They teach all the theoretical and/or practical subjects of the course	
a.2 They teach between 51% and 75% of the course's theoretical subjects	
a.3They teach between 51% and 75% of the course's practical subjects	
a.4They teach between 25% and 50% of the course's theoretical subjects	
a.5They teach between 25% and 50% of the course's practical subjects	
a.6They teach less than 25% of the course subjects (theoretical and/or practical)	

b) Regarding the level of professional training - the number of teachers:

Item	Quantity

b.1 No specific qualification in the course area	
b.2 With technical training	
b.3 With a degree	
b.4 With specialisation	
b.5 With a master's degree	
b.6 With a doctorate	

c) Regarding teaching experience - the number of teachers:

Item		Quantity
c.1	No teaching experience	
c.2	With teaching experience in other subjects (unrelated to the course)	
c.3	With experience as a teacher of theoretical subjects in the area of the course in question	
c.4	With experience as a teacher of theoretical subjects in similar courses	
c.5	Experience teaching practical subjects on similar courses	
c.6	With teaching experience in theoretical subjects combined with practical subjects in similar courses	

d) Course teachers: (mark the alternative(s) with an X)

Item	Option
d.1 They do not participate in the structuring and revisions of the matrix and contents.	
d.2Participate in structuring and revising the matrix and contents.	
d.3They do not participate in the structuring and formatting of didactic material-pedagogy used in the course.	
d.4Participate in the structuring and formatting of didactic-pedagogical material used in the Course	

Part 2 - Profile of the Manager and the Technical and Pedagogical Team

e) Regarding the level of professional training - number of members:

Item	Quantity
e.1 Unqualified	
e.2 With in-service qualification.	
e.3 With secondary and/or technical education	
e.4 With a degree	
e.5 With specialisation	
e.6 With a master's degree	
e.7 With a doctorate	

f) Management (Direction) and Technical Coordination (mark the alternative(s) with an X) The Institution:

Item		Option
f.1	No manager or technical coordinator	
f.2	No manager, but a technical coordinator	
f.3	No technical coordinator, but a manager	
f.4	Has a manager who takes on the role of technical coordinator	

g) Regarding the experience and professional qualifications of the technical coordinator (mark the alternative with an X):

Item	Option
g.1 They have no experience or professional qualifications appropriate to the job and the course	
g.2 They have experience but no professional qualifications appropriate to the course.	
g.3 Has professional experience and qualifications appropriate to the course	

h) Regarding the work of the technical-pedagogical team (mark the alternative(s) with an X)

Item	Option
h.1 The institution does not have a technical-pedagogical team	

h.2 They are indifferent to the course	
h.3 The following are barred from working on the course	
h.4 They provide sporadic support to students and/or teachers on the course.	
h.5 They work in a disjointed way with the management and/or technical coordination, providing support to the students and/or teachers on the course.	
h.6 They only work when requested by the management and/or technical coordination, providing support to the students and teachers on the course.	
h.7 They act in an integrated manner with the management and/or technical coordination, providing constant support to the students and teachers on the course.	

Part 3 - Infrastructure Profile

i) Infrastructure: Physical space and equipment

	Item	Quantity
i.1	Improvised classroom	
i.2	Laboratory unsuitable for the subject	
i.3	Laboratory adequate for the number of students, but lacking the equipment to meet the demands of the subject.	
i.4	The classroom is adequate for the number of students, but lacks the equipment to meet the demands of the course.	
i.5	Classroom suitable for the number of students and equipped to meet the demands of the course	
i.6	Laboratory suitable for the number of students and equipped to meet the demands of the subject	
i.7	Computer room exclusively for the course	
i.8	Library (or study room) exclusively for the course	
i.9	General library	
i.1O	Computer room to cater for all courses	
i.11	Computer room with equipment suitable for the course	
i.12	Up-to-date bibliographic collection that serves the course	

j) Infrastructure: Toilet / changing room (mark alternative(s) with X) The Institution:

	Item	Option
j-1	No bathroom	
j-2	Single toilet (teachers/staff and students)	
j-3	It has a toilet for students and one for staff	
j-4	It has separate toilets by gender for students only.	
í-5	It has gender-segregated toilets for students and staff.	
j-6	It has toilets and a changing room for employees	

k) Infrastructure: Canteen / cafeteria (mark alternative(s) with X) The Institution:

Item	Option
k.1 No canteen	
k.2 No canteen	
k.3 Canteen	
k.4 Cafeteria	
k.5 Cafeteria for employees only	
k.6 Cafeteria for students and staff	
k.7 It has an area reserved for meals for students and staff	

l) Infrastructure: management, coordination and secretariat (mark alternative(s) with X) The Institution:

	Item	Option
1.1	No management room, technical coordination or secretariat	
I.2	Coordination room	
I.3	Has a school office	
I.4	It has a management room	
I.5	It has a management, coordination and secretariat room in the same physical space.	

I.6	It has a co-ordination room and a secretary's room in the same physical space.	
I.7	It has a director's office and a secretary's office in the same physical space.	

List other physical spaces in the institution that cater for the course:

____

____

____

Part 4 - Profile of teaching resources and school organisation

m) Regarding didactic-pedagogical resources (mark the alternative(s) with an X)

Item	Option
m.1 No material available for the course's practical classes	
m.2 No material available for the course lectures	
m.3 There is material available for the course's practical classes, but it is inadequate or insufficient to meet demand	
m.4 There is material available for the course's lectures, but it is inadequate or insufficient to meet demand.	
m.5 Adapted the material to meet the specific demands of the course's theoretical and/or practical classes	
m.6 Developed/acquired material to meet the specific demands of the course's theoretical and practical classes.	

n) Course curriculum and syllabus (mark the alternative(s) with an X) The Course:

Item	Option
n.1 It does not have a curriculum matrix or defined programme contents.	
n.2 It has a curriculum matrix and programme contents, but they do not meet its training profile.	
n.3 It has a curriculum matrix that meets its training profile, but the programme content does not.	
n.4 The syllabus meets the training profile, but the curriculum does not comply with the legislation.	
n.5 It has a curriculum matrix and/or programme content adapted from other courses.	
n.6 Has a curriculum matrix and programme content designed to meet its training profile	

o) The regulations and the pedagogical political project (mark the alternative(s) with an X) The Course:

Item	Option
o.1 Does not have a pedagogical policy project	
o.2 Intends to start building its pedagogical policy project in the next 6 months	
o.3 It is building its political pedagogical project	
o.4 It has its pedagogical policy project, but it is not known by the school community.	
o.5 It has its pedagogical policy project, but it is not reviewed annually by the school community.	
o.6 It has its pedagogical policy project, which is reviewed and implemented by the entire school community.	
.7 No regulations	
0.8 Intends to start building its bylaws in the next 6 months	
o.9 It has bylaws, but they are not distributed to the school community.	
o.10 It has bylaws, which are distributed to the school community.	

Part 5 - Course results profile

p) According to the records in the Final Acts, the retention rate for students on the course was:

Item		Option
p.1	From 90 to 100%	
p.2	From 70 to 89%	
p.3	From 50 to 69%	
p.4	From 30 to 49%	
p.5	From 10 to 29%	
p.6	From 0% to 9%	

q) According to the records in the Final Acts, the dropout rate for students on the course was:

Item		Option
q.1	From 90 to 100%	
q.2	From 70 to 89%	
q.3	From 50 to 69%	
q.4	From 30 to 49%	
q.5	From 10 to 29%	
q.6	From 0% to 9%	

r) According to the records of the Final Acts, the pass rate of the students on the course was:

Item		Option
r.1	From 90 to 100%	
r.2	From 70 to 89%	
r.3	From 50 to 69%	
r.4	From 30 to 49%	
r.5	From 10 to 29%	
r.6	From 0% to 9%	

s) According to the office's records, the number of students who got internships was:

Item		Option
s.1	From 90 to 100%	
s.2	From 70 to 89%	
s.3	From 50 to 69%	
s.4	From 30 to 49%	
s.5	From 10 to 29%	
s.6	From 0% to 9%	

Part 6 - Course implementation cost profile

t) According to management records, the cost of setting up the course was:

u)

Part 7 - Cost profile per class

v) According to the management's records, the cost per course was:

Item		R$
u.1	Educational material	
u.2	Consumables	
u.3	Laboratory equipment	
u.4	Human resources	
u.5	Scholarships (Student Financial Aid)	
u.6	Maintenance	
u.7	Publicity / selection process	
u.8	Consultancy/lectures	
u.9	Transport/ per diems	
u.10	Commercial (Individuals)	
u.11	Services (Legal Entities)	
u.12	Other:	
	Total	

Cost:

- per class: R$
- per student: R$

ANNEX B - Model Questionnaire for Situational Analysis of the Course: Consumer: Teacher

Teacher training:

1. In your opinion, graduates will have employment or income-generating opportunities?Please justify your answer.

2. In your opinion, do the Curricular Matrix and Programme Contents of the Course enable the training of professionals to meet the demands of social agents (private and public companies, NGOs, etc.)? If not, what would need to be changed in order to meet them?

3. In your opinion, does the infrastructure offered by the institution make it possible to train professionals to meet the demands of social agents? If it doesn't, what would need to be changed/invested in so that it does?

4. How do you rate it?

   a. the course curriculum (justify):

   b. the professionals (teachers, technical-pedagogical staff, management, coordination).

5. Did you participate in the conception and/or implementation of the course? How?

6. Suggestions/Criticisms/Comments:

____

____

____

ANNEX C - Model Questionnaire for Situational Analysis of the Course: Consumer: Graduates

1. Are you (or have you been) employed/interning or self-employed in the area of the course you have taken?

2. Are you studying? Which course?

3. What challenges and opportunities did you face after taking the course?

4. In your opinion, do the subjects and contents of the course make it possible to train professionals to meet the needs of the market? If not, what do you think would be necessary?

5. In your opinion, has the infrastructure offered by the institution made it possible for your training to meet the needs of the market? If not, what would need to be changed/invested in so that it does?

6. How do you rate it?

a) the subjects of the course (justify):

b) the professionals (teachers, technical-pedagogical team, management, coordination) who work on the course (justify):

7. What rating do you give to the quality of the teaching provided in the course? (mark only one option with an "X")

Note	Option
Zero	
From 1.0 to 3.9	
From 4.0 to 5.9	
From 6.0 to 7.9	
From 8.0 to 9.9	
Ten	

8. What rating do you give to the institution's infrastructure? (mark only one option with an "X")

Note	Option
Zero	
From 1.0 to 3.9	
From 4.0 to 5.9	
From 6.0 to 7.9	
From 8.0 to 9.9	
Ten	

9. Suggestions/Criticisms/Comments:

____

____

____

ANNEX D - Model Questionnaire for the Productive Segments: Consumer: Representatives of the Productive World

Institution/Company:

Segment:

Total: of employees: Trained in the course area:

1. The offer of vacancies in the area of the Course in question is: internship ( ) employment ( )

2. What is the minimum level of education required to fill these vacancies?

3. Is it difficult to fill vacancies (list some reasons)?

4. Does the company currently have: trainees ( )contractors ( )

5. There is a prospect of hiring trainees: Yes ( ) No ( )

6. Do other companies offer vacancies in this area? Yes ( ) No ( ) I don't know ( )

7. In your opinion, does the profile of the professionals working in your company meet your expectations? Yes ( ) No ( ) I don't know ( )

8. If not, what do you consider to be the right professional profile for the job?

9. What is the desired level of training for professionals working in the area in question?

10. Are you satisfied with the professionals working in your company today?

11. In your opinion, what would need to be added to professional training in order to meet the demands of the service?

12. Of the educational institutions offering the course in question, which one(s) do you consider to be of excellence in training professionals? Why?

MIX
Papier aus verantwortungsvollen Quellen
Paper from responsible sources
FSC® C105338

Printed by Books on Demand GmbH, Norderstedt / Germany